T0212447

Lecture Notes in Computer Science   10084

Commenced Publication in 1973
Founding and Former Series Editors:
Gerhard Goos, Juris Hartmanis, and Jan van Leeuwen

More information about this series at http://www.springer.com/series/7409

Marco X. Bornschlegl · Felix C. Engel
Raymond Bond · Matthias L. Hemmje (Eds.)

Advanced Visual Interfaces

Supporting Big Data Applications

AVI 2016 Workshop, AVI-BDA 2016
Bari, Italy, June 7–10, 2016
Revised Selected Papers

Springer

Editors

Marco X. Bornschlegl
Faculty of Mathematics and Computer
 Science
University of Hagen
Hagen
Germany

Felix C. Engel
Faculty of Mathematics and Computer
 Science
University of Hagen
Hagen
Germany

Raymond Bond
School of Computing and Mathematics
Ulster University
Newtownabbey, Antrim
UK

Matthias L. Hemmje
Faculty of Mathematics and Computer
 Science
University of Hagen
Hagen
Germany

ISSN 0302-9743   ISSN 1611-3349   (electronic)
Lecture Notes in Computer Science
ISBN 978-3-319-50069-0   ISBN 978-3-319-50070-6   (eBook)
DOI 10.1007/978-3-319-50070-6

Library of Congress Control Number: 2016959633

LNCS Sublibrary: SL3 – Information Systems and Applications, incl. Internet/Web, and HCI

Printed on acid-free paper

This Springer imprint is published by Springer Nature
The registered company is Springer International Publishing AG
The registered company address is: Gewerbestrasse 11, 6330 Cham, Switzerland

Preface

This volume contains the full papers presented, discussed, extended, and revised in the context of the 13th Conference on Advanced Visual Interfaces (AVI) 2016 during the Workshop on Road Mapping Infrastructures for Advanced Visual Interfaces Supporting Big Data Applications in Virtual Research Environments held on June 7 in Bari, Italy.

The workshop initializing the work was organized by a collaboration of my fellow colleagues, Marco Xaver Bornschlegl, University of Hagen, Germany, Tiziana Catarci, La Sapienza – Università di Roma, Italy, Andrea Manieri, Engineering Ingegneria Informatica SPA, Italy, Paul Walsh, Cork Institute of Technology, Ireland, and myself in my capacity as Chair of Multimedia and Internet Applications at the Faculty of Mathematics and Computer Science at the University of Hagen. The workshop was produced in the context of the EDISON project that has received funding from the European Union's Horizon 2020 research and innovation program under grant agreement No. 675419. However, this workshop reflects only the author's view and the European Commission is not responsible for any use that may be made of the information it contains.

Handling the complexity of relevant data requires new techniques about data access, visualization, perception, and interaction for supporting innovative and successful information strategies. In order to address human–computer interaction, cognitive efficiency, and interoperability problems, a generic information visualization, user empowerment, as well as service integration and mediation approach based on the existing state of the art in the relevant areas of computer science as well as established open ICT industry standards has to be achieved.

Therefore, this workshop has addressed these issues with a special focus on supporting distributed big data analysis in virtual research environments (VREs). In this way, the purpose of this research road-mapping workshop was threefold. Firstly, it aimed at consolidating information, technical details, and research directions from the diverse range of academic and industrial R&D projects currently available. Secondly, based on visions of future infrastructures, gaps in the current state-of-the-art reference models were determined and thirdly, a new reference model was derived and validated. To achieve these aims the workshop brought together researchers and practitioners who are able to contribute to and aid in the research road-mapping, in the deriving and validating of a corresponding reference model, and in supporting a corresponding set of publications based on their work as well as on a reflection of their own work along the road-mapping results represented by means of the derived reference model for the target infrastructure. The results of this road-mapping activity and the corresponding reference model can be used to inform, influence, and disseminate ideas to the wider research community.

In consequence, the Call for Papers of the workshop invited contributions from academic and industrial researchers and practitioners working in the area of big data visualization. The ten initial submissions of position papers from five different countries were carefully reviewed by at least three Program Committee members.

Based on submitted position papers and existing research, the workshop outlined the current baseline of infrastructures for advanced visual user interfaces supporting big data applications in VREs. Furthermore, it outlined research gaps that need to be filled for achieving the targeted research and development ambitions. Achievement of the goal of the workshop was supported by the presentation and discussion of research aiming at delivering advanced visual user interfaces for VREs, e.g., supporting researchers and organizations in applying and maintaining distributed (spatially, physically, as well as potentially cross-organizational and cross-domain) research resources for big data analysis. These advanced visual user interfaces can, e.g., provide a basis for managing access to VRE features and services through open standards and they can be materialized through an open architecture and components derived from state-of-the-art research results being able to deal with big data resources and services at scale. In this way, the resulting research road-mapping and the corresponding derived reference model can pave the way toward collaborating on the development of a visual user interface tool suite supporting VRE platforms that can host big data analysis and corresponding research activities sharing distributed research resources by adopting common existing open standards for access, analysis, and visualization. Thereby, this research road-mapping and corresponding validated reference model helps realizing a ubiquitous collaborative workspace for researchers, which is able to facilitate the research process and its big data analysis applications.

The workshop was performed during a full day and was structured in four sessions to provide maximum time for group discussion and brainstorming. In the first session the participants briefly introduced themselves with short five-minute talks. Following this, the workshop presented a series of invited industry and eScience-infrastructure research community perspectives. In the third session, a gap analysis and validation were completed on the basis of each research domain perspective presented and on the basis of the derived reference model. In the fourth session the group summarized the gaps and set forth the timeline and areas for completing their corresponding full publications in order to reflect the gaps and fully validate the derived reference model. The workshop ended with a detailed discussion to define immediate next steps for completing the corresponding validation of the reference model based on transforming the initial position papers into full publications capturing the results of the road-mapping discussions in the workshop. In addition, comments of several external reviewers for these full publications of the workshop outcome were also sought.

I would like to thank all the authors for contributing high-quality research position papers to the workshop and full papers as well as for the revisions of these full papers after an additional review to establish the content for these proceedings. I would also like to express my sincere thanks to the Organizing and Program Committee, to the members of my Editorial Board, as well as the all the additional external reviewers for reviewing the papers within a very short period of time. We also thank Springer for publishing the proceedings in the *Lecture Notes in Computer Science* series.

September 2016   Matthias L. Hemmje

Organization

Organization Committee

Marco Xaver Bornschlegl	University of Hagen, Germany
Tiziana Catarci	La Sapienza – Università di Roma, Italy
Matthias L. Hemmje	University of Hagen, Germany
Andrea Manieri	Engineering Ingegneria Informatica SPA, Italy
Paul Walsh	Cork Institute of Technology, Ireland

Program Committee

Themis Athanassiadou	EGI.eu, The Netherlands
Adam Belloum	University of Amsterdam, The Netherlands
Marco Xaver Bornschlegl	University of Hagen, Germany
Paolo Buono	Università degli Studi di Bari, Italy
Tiziana Catarci	Università di Roma, Italy
Maria Francesca Costabile	Università degli Studi di Bari, Italy
Matthias L. Hemmje	University of Hagen, Germany
Boro Jakimovski	Ss. Cyril and Methodius University in Skopje, R. Macedonia
Michael Kaufmann	Lucerne University of Applied Sciences and Arts, Switzerland
Andrea Manieri	Engineering Ingegneria Informatica SPA, Italy
Massimo Mecella	Università di Roma, Italy
Ruben Riestra	Groupo INMARK, Spain
Paul Walsh	Cork Institute of Technology, Ireland
Tomasz Wiktorski	University of Stavanger, Norway
Huiru Zheng	University of Ulster, UK

Additional Reviewers

Andrew Cairns	Ulster University, UK
Brian Davis	NUI Galway, Ireland
Julie Doyle	Dundalk Institute of Technology, Ireland
Stephen Gallagher	Ulster University, UK
Alfie Keary	Cork Institute of Technology, Ireland
Jun Liu	Ulster University, UK
Paul McCullagh	Ulster University, UK
Maurice Mulvenna	Ulster University, UK

Chris Porter   University of Malta, Malta
Gavin Robert Sim   University of Central Lancashire, UK
Haiying Wang   Ulster University, UK
Mathieu Zen   Université Catholique de Louvain, France

Contents

IVIS4BigData: A Reference Model for Advanced Visual Interfaces Supporting Big Data Analysis in Virtual Research Environments

Marco X. Bornschlegl[1][(✉)], Kevin Berwind[1], Michael Kaufmann[2],
Felix C. Engel[1], Paul Walsh[3], Matthias L. Hemmje[1], and Ruben Riestra[4]

[1] Faculty of Mathematics and Computer Science,
University of Hagen, Hagen, Germany
{marco-xaver.bornschlegl,kevin.berwind,
felix.engel,matthias.hemmje}@fernuni-hagen.de
[2] Lucerne University of Applied Sciences and Arts, Engineering and Architecture,
Horw, Switzerland
m.kaufmann@hslu.ch
[3] CIT Informatics, Cork Institute of Technology, Cork, Ireland
paul.walsh@cit.ie
[4] Grupo INMARK, Madrid, Spain
ruben.riestra@grupoinmark.com

Abstract. This paper introduces an approach to develop an up-to-date reference model that can support advanced visual user interfaces for distributed Big Data Analysis in virtual labs to be used in e-Science, industrial research, and Data Science education. The paper introduces and motivates the current situation in this application area as a basis for a corresponding problem statement that is utilized to derive goals and objectives of the approach. Furthermore, the relevant state-of-the-art is revisited and remaining challenges are identified. An exemplar set of use cases, corresponding user stereotypes as well as a conceptual design model to address these challenges are introduced. A corresponding architectural system model is suggested as a conceptual reference architecture to support proof-of-concept implementations as well as to support interoperability in distributed infrastructures. Conclusions and an outlook on future work complete the paper.

Keywords: Advanced visual user interfaces · Distributed Big Data Analysis · Information visualization · User empowerment · Virtual Research Environments

1 Introduction and Motivation

The availability of data has changed dramatically over the past ten years. The wide distribution of web-enabled mobile devices and the evolution of web 2.0 technologies are contributing to a large amount of data (so-called Big Data) [29]. Usable access to complex and large amounts of data poses, e.g., an immense challenge

M.X. Bornschlegl et al. (Eds.): AVI-BDA 2016, LNCS 10084, pp. 1–18, 2016.
DOI: 10.1007/978-3-319-50070-6_1

for current solutions in, e.g., Business Analytics. Handling the complexity of relevant data (generated through information deluge and being targeted with Big Data technologies) requires new techniques about data access, visualization, perception, and interaction for innovative and successful strategies. As a consequence research communities as well as industry, but especially research teams at small universities and **Small and Medium-sized Enterprises (SMEs)**, will be faced with enormous challenges. Furthermore, current e-Science research resources and infrastructures (i.e., data, tools, and related **Information and Communication Technology (ICT)** services) are often confined to computer science expert usage only and fail to leverage the abundant opportunities that distributed, dynamic, and eventually interdisciplinary **Virtual Research Environments (VREs)** can provide to scientists, industrial research users as well as to learners in computer science, data science and related educational environments.

This trend calls for innovative, dynamic and ubiquitous research supporting VREs where scattered scientists can seamlessly access data, software, and processing resources managed by diverse systems in separate administration domains through their web browser [11]. Therefore, nowadays a VRE allows researchers from all disciplines to work collaboratively by managing the increasingly complex range of tasks involved in carrying out research on both small and large scales [18,33]. However, these VREs lack cognitive efficient and effective **Human-Computer Interaction (HCI)** support and overall interoperability in existing approaches. In detail this means, VREs lack standardized and user-centered access to as well as cognitive efficient configuration, management, and usage of research resources during the execution of collaborative research processes where intermediate results have to be shared between interdisciplinary teams and their organizations. Furthermore, they lack a generic and user-centered service infrastructure supporting the entire life cycle of VREs, like cognitive efficient interactive/visually direct manipulative set-up, configuration, integration, management, and usage of existing research resources. Finally, they lack instructional support on how to create, configure, deploy, manage and collaborate. In order to address human-computer interaction, cognitive efficiency, and interoperability problems, a generic information visualization, user empowerment, as well as service integration and mediation approach based on the existing state-of-the-art in the relevant areas of computer science as well as established open ICT standards has to be achieved. This paper will address these issues with a special focus on supporting distributed Big Data analysis in VREs.

The overall goal of this research is to develop a reference model that can support advanced visual user interfaces for distributed Big Data Analysis in virtual labs to be used in e-Science, industrial research, and data science education. The surrounding infrastructure will support the life cycle of VREs by enabling the dynamic ad-hoc definition of new interdisciplinary research projects within advanced visual user interface supporting cognitive efficiency as well as user empowerment. In this way, this research will create a visual user interface tool suite supporting a VRE platform infrastructure that can host Big Data Analysis and corresponding research activities sharing distributed research resources (i.e., data, tools, and services) by adopting common existing open standards for access, analysis and visualization, realizing an ubiquitous collaborative workspace for researchers which is able to facilitate the research process and its Big Data Analysis applications.

2   State of the Art

The terms **data**, **information**, and **knowledge** are often used in processes, tools, and applications within the computer science fields of information systems, knowledge technologies, and knowledge management. Ackoff [1] differentiated data, information, and knowledge based on the following definitions: *"Data is raw. It simply exists and has no significance beyond its existence (in and of itself). It can exist in any form, usable or not. It does not have meaning of itself. Information is data that has been given meaning by way of relational connection. Knowledge is the appropriate collection of information, such that it's intent is to be useful. Knowledge is a deterministic process and transforms information into instructions."* Kuhlen [40] deduces information not only from contextualized data, but rather from knowledge as well, because *"knowledge must be represented in any way, for the simple reason that there is no existing way for direct interchange of ideas at present"* [40]. He defines information as an *"referential and pragmatical concept, which refers to underlying knowledge and its relevance only gains by a recent decision or a current action context"* [40]. Relating to the differences between knowledge and information, Nonaka and Takeuchi [43] highlighted that, firstly, knowledge is about beliefs and commitment as it is a function of a particular perspective. Secondly, knowledge is about action, that is, knowledge achieves some end. Consequently, a distinction is made that knowledge is a more complex form of information [36]. Furthermore, they segmented knowledge into two dimensions. A technical dimension (**explicit knowledge**), which includes all the knowledge already explicitly available in documentations and publications or any other kind of already externalized and therefore informally or formally encoded media objects and an important cognitive dimension (**tacit knowledge**), which encompasses the kind of informal and *"hard-to-pin-down"* skills [43].

Data Mining (DM), **Business Intelligence (BI)** and **Knowledge Management (KM)** are often considered together as necessarily integrated and mutually critical components in the management of intellectual capital [35]. Nevertheless, these three concepts differ in some respects. Palace [46] describes DM as *"a process of analyzing data from different perspectives and summarizing it into useful information, [...] which allows users to analyze data from many different dimensions or angles, categorize it, and summarize the relationships identified."* In contrast to DM which is focusing on looking forward in order to support organizations in anticipating in what is coming, to change the business and move forward, BI and KM are using historical data to tell organizations what happened and what is needed to run the business [49]. Nevertheless, while both BI and KM are focusing on the insights to support management functions in industry in their decision making process, they differ in the type of raw materials used, the processes to develop knowledge, and the type of knowledge developed [44]. Saggion et al. [50] describe BI as a process of finding, gathering, aggregating and analyzing information for decision-making. It makes use of a set of technologies that allow the acquisition and analysis of data to improve company decision making and work flows [35]. Finally, Gartner [30] defines KM as *"a business process that formalizes the management and use of an enterprise's intellectual assets."* KM promotes a collaborative and integrative approach to the creation, capture, organization, access and use of information assets, including the tacit, uncaptured knowledge of people. According to Garter, Hameed [32] describes KM as a systematic process of finding, selecting, organizing, distilling and presenting information in a way that improves an employee's comprehension in a specific area of interest which supports an organization to gain insight and understanding from its own experience.

Providing integrated access to multiple heterogeneous information/knowledge sources for constructing synthesized and uniform knowledge resource descriptions with uniform query interfaces against the information sources is a big challenge [6]. An attempt that is made to combine these diverse sources of data by using semantic standards, that are embedded inside these data sources, such as an ontology, which describes concepts and relations for representing and defining a specific knowledge domain, is **Semantic Integration (SI)**. In semantic approaches of data integration, a **Mediator-Wrapper Architecture (MWA)** is often used to perform this operation. This MWA, illustrated in Fig. 1 and first mentioned by Wiederhold [57], has been widely accepted for solving information integration problems, especially for Web based application development [51].

Wrappers are developed for each kind of data representation [6] and used to provide access to heterogeneous data sources. For each data source, a wrapper exports some information about its schema, data and query processing capabilities. A mediator, a *"software module that exploits encoded knowledge about certain sets or subsets of data to create information for a higher layer of applications"* [57], stores the information provided by wrappers in a unified view (e.g. performed with semantic integration) of all available data with central data

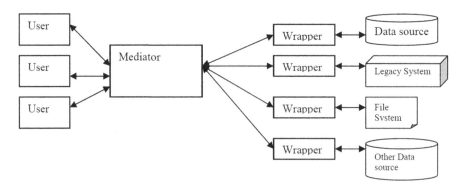

Fig. 1. Mediator-Wrapper Architecture [45,51]

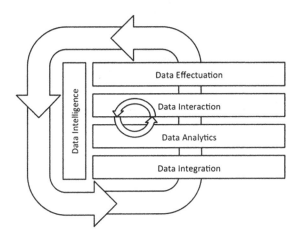

Fig. 2. Reference model for BDM [37]

dictionary. It decomposes the user query in smaller queries that can be executed by wrappers, gathers the results from wrappers and creates answers to the user query [51].

Kaufmann [37] describes **Big Data Management (BDM)** as *"the process of optimally controlling flows of large-volume, high-velocity, heterogeneous and uncertain data."* Usually, Big Data is approached with a technological focus, but a key question for businesses is how Big Data can be effectively used to create value. Therefore in this model, as illustrated in Fig. 2, the classical technological aspects of Big Data (cf., e.g., Singh and Reddy [53]), namely **Data Integration** (i.e. Hadoop [2] clusters NoSQL databases and other database management systems) and **Data Analytics** (i.e. statistical, machine learning and data mining tools and techniques) are complemented by three additional layers, called **Data Interaction, Data Effectuation** and **Data Intelligence**, to improve the effective benefit of Big Data technologies.

On top of the two basic layers, which are focusing on data technology, there is a layer called **Data Interaction** to illustrate the importance of human-computer interaction in the process for BDM, which is defined as a key aspect in this model. In this step, human decision makers are getting in touch with analysis results to view, manipulate, correct and communicate them. Conversely, data are getting in touch with the users of the information system, creating a bi-directional interaction between technology and its users, as symbolized by the small feedback loop. Nevertheless, interacting with analysis results is not sufficient to create actual value from data. For the optimization of business objectives, according to Davenport [23], it is necessary that the effects of data analysis are integrated with products and services of an organization. Therefore, another layer called **Data Effectuation** is defined, in which value creation from data is addressed. Finally, the model describes a cross-sectional function of knowledge-based processes and technologies which support the big data management life cycle. Value creation

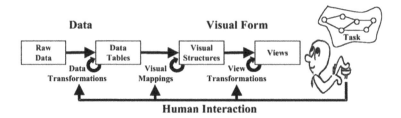

Fig. 3. IVIS reference model [16]

from data depends highly on emergent knowledge processes in the organization (Markus, Majchrzak, and Gasser [41]; Patel and Ghoneim [47]). The layer called **Data Intelligence** ought to ensure that knowledge and skills can be acquired and properly managed in the context of Big Data management. Kaufmann [37] proposes to apply KM and **Knowledge Engineering (KE)** techniques to all layers of the BDM from integration to effectuation, for example, by archiving and semantically annotating analysis results, by optimally communicating data-based insights, or by actively managing data science know-how.

Information Visualization (IVIS) has emerged *"from research in human-computer interaction, computer science, graphics, visual design, psychology, and business methods"* [54]. Nevertheless, IVIS can also be seen as a result of the question for interchanging ideas and information between human, keeping with Rainer Kuhlen [40], because of the missing direct way. The most precise and common definition of IVIS as *"the use of computer-supported, interactive, visual representations of abstract data to amplify cognition"* stems from Card et al. [16]. To simplify the discussion about information visualization systems and to compare and contrast them, Card et al. [16] defined a reference model, which is illustrated in Fig. 3, for mapping data to visual forms for human perception.

In this model, arrows lead from **Raw Data** to visual data presentation of the raw data within a cognitive efficient IVIS based on a **Visual Structure** and its rendering of a view that is easy to perceive and interact with for humans. The arrows in this model indicate a series of data transformations whereas each arrow might indicate multiple chained transformations. Moreover, additional arrows from the human at the right into the transformations themselves indicate the adjustment of these transformations by user-operated controls supporting human-computer interaction [16]. **Data Transformations** map raw data such as text data, processing information, (database-) tables, e-mails, feeds and sensor data into **Data Tables** which define the data with relational descriptions and extended meta data [5,29]. **Visual Mappings** transform data tables into visual structures, that combine spatial substrates, marks and graphical properties. Finally, **View Transformations** create views of the visual structures by specifying graphical parameters such as position, scaling and clipping [16]. *"Although raw data can be visualized directly, data tables are an important step when the data are abstract, without a direct spatial component"* [16]. Therefore, Card et al. define the mapping of a data table to a visual structure, i.e. a visual mapping, as the core of reference model, this operation translates the mathematical relations within data tables to **Graphical Properties** within visual structures.

Whereas the purpose of IVIS is insight [16,52] the purpose of **Visual Analytics (VA)** is to enable and discover insight [20,55]. To be more precise, Wong et al. [58] defines VA as *"a contemporary and proven approach to combine the art of human intuition and the science of mathematical deduction to directly perceive patterns and derive knowledge and insight from them"*. On a grand scale, VA solutions provide technology that combines the advantages of machines with strengths of humans. While methods from statistics and mathematics are the driving force on the automatic analysis side, capabilities to perceive, relate and conclude turn VA into a very promising field of research [28,38,39].

Current development leads to a continuous growth of both computer systems and end-user population [22]. Thus, designing visual interfaces for HCI supporting VA requires a critical decision which of the involved parties - the user or the software - will control the interaction. Fischer [26] emphasizes that *"people and tasks are different."* Moreover, he explains that humans start from a partial specification of a task, and refine it incrementally, on the basis of the feedback that they get from their environment. Thus, *"users must be able to articulate incrementally the task at hand. The information provided in response to these problem-solving activities based on partial specifications and constructions must assist users to refine the definition of their problem"* [26]. To turn computers into convivial tools, to underpin the evolution of end users from passive information consumers into information producers, requires that people can use, change and enhance their tools and build new ones without having to become professional-level programmers [3,25]. In order to design successful interactive systems that meet users' expectations and improve their daily life, Costabile et al. [22] consider a two-phase process. The first phase being designing the design environment (meta-design phase), which refers to the design of environments that allows end users to be actively involved in the continuous development use and evolution of systems, the second one being designing the applications by using the design environment. All stakeholders of an interactive system, including end users, are "owners" of a part of the problem: Software engineers know the technology, end users know the application domain, Human-Computer Interaction experts know human factors, etc.; they must all contribute to system design by bringing their own expertise [22].

A **Virtual Research Environment (VRE)** which allows multiple researchers in different locations to work together in real time without restrictions was firstly described by UK's **Joint Information Systems Committee (JISC)** *VRE Collaborative Landscape Study* in 2010 [18] as *"a platform, to help researchers from all disciplines to work collaboratively by managing the increasingly complex range of tasks involved in carrying out research on both small and large scales"* [18,33].

From a technological perspective, VREs are based primarily on software services and communication networks. In terms of content, VREs potentially support the entire research process - from the collection, discussion, and further processing of data right through to the publication of results. Virtual Research Environments are essential components of state-of-the-art research infrastructures [33]. Traditionally, most VREs are statically defined technology stacks created for silos of research. In contrast, by explicitly implementing this life cycle model, the approach arms at realizing the concept of software defined architectures whereby any kind of researchers can define and deploy VREs dynamically to meet their needs.

3   Related Work

3.1   Open Science Framework

"Though most scientists believe in the ideals of openness, transparency, and reproducibility, the reality is that the incentive structure of academic research encourages exactly the opposite" [17]. Scientists have a strong profession to get their results published, but science is still a pretty closed and exclusive system where most results end up being published in prestigious closed journals which many researchers, as well as the publicity around the world, cannot access [17]. Moreover, *"many scientists are stuck with outdated and closed source tools that aren't up to the task of managing their increasingly complicated workflows"* [17].

Based on the success that an inclusive approach has brought to the Python Community [48], the **Center for Open Science (COS)**, *"a non-profit technology startup founded in 2013 with a mission to increase openness, integrity, and reproducibility of scientific research"* [19], seized on this approach and developed a software where science can benefit from the values of openness and inclusivity [17]. Therefore, with the **Open Science Framework (OSF)** [19] a free and open source web application that connects and supports the research workflow, they aim to enable scientists to increase the efficiency and effectiveness of their research [19]. The various capabilities of the OSF application addressing a wide range of academic and industrial use case scenarios, where:

– *"**Researchers** can use the OSF to manage their projects and collaborations or register their studies"* [19].
– *"**Academic Meetings and Conferences** can use OSF for meetings to share the posters and slides presented at the conference with a broader audience to increase the impact of the work"* [19].
– *"**Journals** can use the OSF to support data and materials sharing initiatives, or the OSF registry to support preregistration of research"* [19].
– *"**Institutions** can use OSF for Institutions to provide their researchers with a free, open source scholarly commons. Institutional branding and authentication provide a seamless user experience"* [19].
– *"**Funders** can use the OSF to support data and materials sharing initiatives or mandates, to broaden the impact of the work they fund"* [19].

OSF can be used to share manuscripts, unpublished findings, materials, as well as in progress work where all of the work is preserved and easily accessible to only those people that should have access and all of the researchers are working with the correct, up-to-date files [19]. Moreover, OSF makes all of the work citable, that the researchers can have impact and get credit [19].

3.2 gCube

"Scientists have been rethinking research workflows in favour of innovative paradigms to support multidisciplinary, computationally-heavy and data-intensive collaborative activities" [13]. E-Infrastructures supporting Virtual Research Environments, with seamless and on demand access to computation, content, as well as to application services, can play an important role in supporting data enrapturing and curation as well as data analysis and visualization [13,14]. For this reason, as a result of the collaborative efforts of more than 48 researchers and developers in twelve different academic and industrial research centers [14], with gCube [31] the gCube Consortium designed a service-oriented application framework that supports the on-demand sharing of resources for computation, content and application services [14]. Therefore, gCube *"enables scientists to declaratively and dynamically build transient VREs by aggregating and deploying on-demand content resources, application services and computing resources"* [12].

The gCube Framework enables the realization of e-infrastructures that support the notion of VREs, i.e. collaborative digital environments through which scientists, addressing common research challenges, exchange information and produce new knowledge [14]. Moreover, gCube provides mechanisms to easily create dedicated Web portals through which the content and services can be accessed and finally it also monitors the shared resources during the lifetime of the VRE, guaranteeing their optimal allocation and exploitation [12,14].

From the technological point of view, the gCube core is organized in four main areas (**Core Services, Collaboration Services, Data Processing Services, and Data Space Management Services**) that are controlling the whole lifecycle of the provided application [4]. The additional layer of **Resource Providers** supports the gCube core for exploiting a grid-enabled infrastructure and hosting Web Services on it [14].

Whereas the Core Services are providing basic facilities for resource management, security, and VRE management, the Data Space Management Services offers an array of solutions for heterogeneous data types (formats, typologies, semantics) that are possibly falling under the Big Data umbrella in context of a VRE [4]. The Data Processing Services are providing services for the different processing tasks atop of the managed datasets, and the Collaborative Services offer and provide the users of the VRE with added value services for collaboration [4].

"gCube as a whole is a unique system since it covers the entire spectrum of facilities needed to deliver scientific applications as-a-Service" [4]. With its utilization to operate the D4Science.org [21] infrastructure, that offers a number of services and virtual research environments for users willing to acquire concrete understanding of the major features and capabilities [21], *"gCube demonstrates*

that the principles governing the VREs delivery and the system openness are key in the modern science settings" [15].

4   Conceptual Modeling

As illustrated in Fig. 4, Big Data Analysis supporting emerging knowledge generation and innovation-oriented decision making is based on different perspectives and intentions. To support management functions in their ability of making sustainable decisions, Big Data Analysis specialists are filling the gap between Big Data Analysis result consumers and Big Data technologies. Thus, these specialists need to understand their consumers/customers intentions as well as a strong technology watch, but are not equal to developers, because they care about having impact on the business [56].

Deduced from this perspectives and intentions, there are different use cases and user stereotypes that can be identified for performing Big Data analysis collaboratively within an organization seeking to support emerging knowledge generation and innovation. Users with the highest organizational knowledge and competence levels like, e.g., managers of different hierarchy levels of such organizations, need to interact with visual analysis results for their decision making processes. On the other hand, users with low organizational knowledge and competence levels, like system owners or administrators, need to interact directly with data sources, data streams or data tables for operating, customizing or manipulating their systems and contents. Nevertheless, user stereotypes with lower organizational knowledge and competence levels are interested in visualization techniques as well, in case these techniques are focusing on their lower organizational knowledge and competence levels. Finally, there are user stereotype perspectives in the middle of those levels, representing the connection between

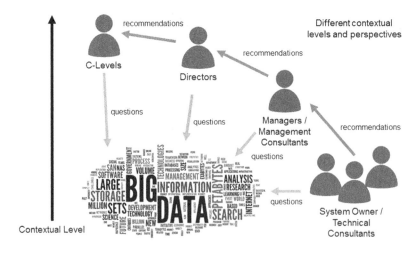

Fig. 4. Big Data Perspectives in Industry [7]

user stereotypes with low and high contextual knowledge and competence levels. Business Analysts or Business Intelligence Consultants in consultancy scenarios are filling the gap between Big Data consumers and Big Data technologies and often interact with both, low level data streams and visualization technologies. As a consequence from these various perspectives and contextual knowledge and competence levels, it is important to provide the different user stereotypes with a kind of context aware information technology infrastructure to support their individual use cases. *"The 'right' information, at the 'right' time, in the 'right' place, in the 'right' way to the 'right' person"* [27]. One could add to this citation *"with the right competences"* or *"with the right user empowerment"*.

As a response to increased graphics performance in computing technologies and information visualization, Card et al. [16] developed the IVIS reference model. Due to further developments in information systems as well as knowledge management systems in recent years, this model has to be adapted for covering the recent advancements. Modern cloud technologies and distributed computing technologies are leading to almost unlimited storage and computing performance. Moreover, usable access to complex and large amounts of data over several data sources requires new techniques for accessing and visualizing data with innovative and successful strategies, at the border between automated data analysis, research insight, and business innovation decision making [28]. Being not in full alignment with these new required techniques, the original IVIS Reference Model only supports transforming data from a single data source on the left directly to a visual representation for the end user on the right, without a direct view and interaction possibility in the single process stages.

Thus, the hybridly refined and extended IVIS4BigData Reference Model [8] (cf. Fig. 5), an adaptation and extension of the original IVIS Reference Model, in combination with Kaufmann's Big **Data Management (BDM)** Reference Model [37] was achieved to cover the new conditions of the present situation with advanced visual interface opportunities for perceiving, managing, and interpreting Big Data analysis results to support insight, emerging knowledge generation and informed decision making. In this way, the derived model became integrated with the underlying reference model for BDM which illustrates different stages of BDM. This means, the adaptation of the IVIS Reference Model represents the interactive part of the underlying BDM life cycle.

According to Card et al., functions which indicate a series of (multiple) data transformations lead from raw data to data presentation for humans. However, instead of collecting raw data from a single data source, multiple interdisciplinary cross-domain and cross-organizational data sources have nowadays to be connected, integrated by means of appropriate information integration approaches like mediator wrapper architectures, and in this way globally managed in **Data Collections** inside the **Data Collection, Management & Curation** layer. Therefore, the first consecutive transformation which is located in the **Analytics** layer of the underlying BDM model, maps the data from the connected data sources into **Data Structures** which represent the first stage in the **Interaction & Perception** layer. The generic term **Data Structures** also includes the use of modern

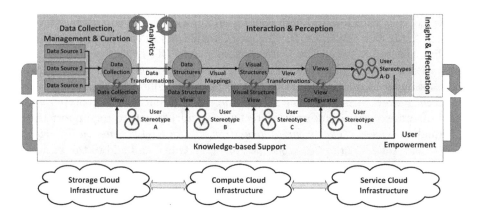

Fig. 5. IVIS4BigData reference model

Big Data Storage Technologies (like, e.g., NoSQL, RDBMS, HDFS), instead of using only data tables with relational schemata. In the following step **Visual Mappings** which transform data tables into **Visual Structures** and **View Transformations** which create **Views** of the **Visual Structures** by specifying graphical parameters such as position, scaling, and clipping, do not differ from the original IVIS reference model. As a consequence, only interacting with analysis results does not lead to any *"added value"* for the optimization of, e.g., research results or business objectives. Furthermore, no process steps are currently located within the **Insight & Effectuation** layer because such *"added value"* is rather generated from knowledge, which is a *"function of a particular perspective"* [43] and will be generated within this layer by combining the analysis results with existing knowledge.

Therefore, the major adaptations are located between the cross-functional **Knowledge-Based Support** layer and the corresponding layers above. As a consequence from the various perspectives and contextual levels of Big Data analysis and management user stereotypes, additional visual interaction features lead from the human users on the right into multiple visually-interactive user interface **Views**. These functional arrows are illustrating the visually directmanipulative interaction between user stereotypes with single process stages and the adjustments of the respective transformations by user-operated user interface controls to provide *"the 'right' information, at the 'right' time, in the 'right' place, in the 'right' way to the 'right' person"* [27] within a context aware and user-empowering system for individual use cases. Finally, the circular iteration around the whole set of layers clarifies that IVIS4BigData is not aiming at supporting solely an one time process because the results can be used as the input for a new process iteration.

5   A Conceptual VRE System Architecture Supporting Proof-of-Concept Implementation

To support researchers and organizations maintaining research resources, a proof-of-concept reference implementation of our IVIS4BigData model will be implemented, by developing an interoperable, cognitive efficient and user empowering VRE infrastructure. As illustrated in Fig. 6, the infrastructure is based on providing and managing access though open standards and is materialized though existing open components procured from successful research projects dealing with resources at scale, and supported by their owners as project partners.

It is building on the concept of semantic information integration and mediation and corresponding mediator architectures to support information integration across borders of scientific knowledge domains. In this way digital research resources from different scientific disciplines can be mediated by means of semantic integration of domain models on the level of the mediator and by means of domain adaptation on the level of the corresponding wrappers. This means, information integration concept is independent of media types and persistency platforms. Moreover, the infrastructure builds on the concepts and service model of **Infrastructure as a Service (IaaS)** Clouds exploiting its scalability, elasticity, self-service, and accounting capabilities as defined by NIST [42]. Finally, it will establish a scientific collaboration model within its VREs that is building on **Computer Supported Collaborative Work (CSCW)** concepts of

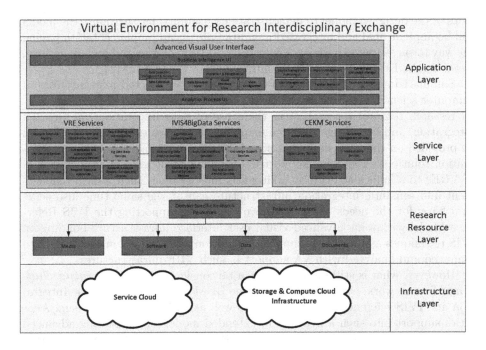

Fig. 6. Conceptual architecture for a VRE infrastructure

configuring, using, and dissolving such VREs in a very controlled way that is at the same time very intuitive, i.e. user-centered and focusing on cognitive efficiencies and attractive user experiences. Thus, it lowers barriers of adoption by harmonizing these offerings with a cloud infrastructure for service delivery and provides services for the secure collaborative management of interdisciplinary research projects in VREs with a comprehensive set of standard-based services, interfaces, and tools that support their complete life cycle in a domain agnostic fashion.

6   Discussion and Outlook

The use case scenarios, user stereotypes, as well as the conceptual model were already validated during presentations and discussions in an expert round table with experts from European e-Science and e-Infrastructure research institutions during the EGI community forum conference 2015 [34], as well as during the AVI 2016 conference [10] workshop *Road Mapping Infrastructures for Advanced Visual Interfaces Supporting Big Data Applications in Virtual Research Environments* [9]. The evaluation approach of the developed model will be conducted with two different strategies. The first strategy will use case study research to answer the needs of Big Data user stereotypes. In addition to the case study evaluation, the second evaluation strategy will use the outcomes of existing research literature of the underlying models. Based on their scientific popularity, the advantages and disadvantages will be compared in conjunction to the characteristics of the designed model to demonstrate its usability. Furthermore, the model will be implemented and integrated in a proof-of-concept implementation paving the way towards user experiments with the EGI technologies and infrastructures, based on the EGI Federated Cloud infrastructure (Fed-Cloud [24]).

Summarizing our initial state-of-the-art review in selected relevant areas of computer science, it can be stated that a sufficient method for supporting overall research resource integration in the sense of data integration, information integration, and knowledge resource mapping and access support for VREs can be provided on the basis of mediator architectures implementing semantic integration solutions. These can support data management aspects and challenges of VREs to a sufficient degree. Taking this into account, such a data management and semantic integration infrastructure can at the same time also serve as a basis for the needs of the first two phases of supporting the IVIS Reference Model within an advanced visual user interface infrastructure building on IVIS techniques as a means to support perception and interaction with Big Data managed and analyzed with VA support in such VRE infrastructures.

However, what is still missing and can be considered as a ***remaining challenge*** for our work, is an integration of the BDM model with Semantic Integration and IVIS reference infrastructures as well as an integration of Visual Analytics support into such a hybrid and extended model for supporting advanced visual interfaces for Big Data analysis in VREs. Furthermore, from the point of view of user empowerment, an identification of use cases and corresponding user stereotypes for utilizing such advanced visual interfaces for Big Data analysis in VREs remains as an additional challenge. This means, that first of all such different user stereotypes have to be derived from representative use cases and then appropriate user empowerment methods have to be designed depending on an analysis of the skills and competences of the different user stereotypes. In the remainder of this paper we will therefore work on the establishment of an identification of initial use cases, an initial identification of user stereotypes for user empowerment related to these use cases, as well as the design of a hybrid model integrating the BDM Reference Model with the IVIS Reference Model and visual analysis support. In this way we can come up with on the one hand a basis for later deriving specifications of process models and information models that can be processed within architectures of such infrastructures and that can drive advanced visual interfaces supporting Big Data analysis within VREs. On the other hand, we can use these use cases, user stereotypes and integrated reference model to derive a conceptual architecture that can support such processes and information models which identifies another important remaining challenge.

Acknowledgments and Disclaimer. This publication has been produced in the context of the EDISON project. The project has received funding from the European Union's Horizon 2020 research and innovation programme under grant agreement No 675419. However, this paper reflects only the author's view and the European Commission is not responsible for any use that may be made of the information it contains.

References

1. Ackoff, R.: From data to wisdom. J. Appl. Syst. Anal. **16**, 3–9 (1989)
2. Apache Software Foundation: Apache hadoop (version: 2.6.3) (2014). https:// hadoop.apache.org. Accessed 10 Jan 2016
3. Ardito, C., Buono, P., Costabile, M.F., Lanzilotti, R., Piccinno, A.: End users as co-designers of their own tools and products. J. Visual Lang. Comput. **23**(2), 78– 90 (2012). http://dx.doi.org/10.1016/j.jvlc.2011.11.005. Special issue dedicated to Prof. Piero Mussio
4. Assante, M., Cancela, L., Castelli, D., Coro, G., Lelii, L., Pagano, P.: Virtual research environments as-a-service by gcube. In: Proceedings of the 8th International Workshop on Science Gateways (IWSG 2016), IWSG 2016 (2016)
5. Beath, C., Becerra-Fernandez, I., Ross, J., Short, J.: Finding value in the information explosion. MIT Sloan Manage. Rev. **53**(4), 18 (2012)
6. Bergamaschi, S., Castano, S., Vincini, M.: Semantic integration of semi-structured and structured data sources. SIGMOD Rec. **28**(1), 54–59 (1999). http://doi.acm.org/10.1145/309844.309897
7. Bornschlegl, M.X.: Data science competences to understand big data analysis from a management perspective - a top down view -. In: Hemmje et al. [34]

8. Bornschlegl, M.X., Berwind, K., Kaufmann, M., Hemmje, M.L.: Towards a reference model for advanced visual interfaces supporting big data analysis. In: ICOMP 2016 : The 17th International Conference on Internet Computing and Internet of Things. Global Science and Technology Forum, Las Vegas, Nevada, USA (2016)
9. Bornschlegl, M.X., Manieri, A., Walsh, P., Catarci, T., Hemmje, M.L.: Road mapping infrastructures for advanced visual interfaces supporting big data applications in virtual research environments. In: Buono et al. [10], pp. 363–367. http://doi.acm.org/10.1145/2909132.2927471
10. Buono, P., Lanzilotti, R., Matera, M., Costabile, M.F. (eds.) Proceedings of the International Working Conference on Advanced Visual Interfaces, AVI 2016, Bari, Italy, June 7–10, 2016. ACM (2016). http://doi.acm.org/10.1145/2909132
11. Candela, L.: Virtual research environments. Technical report, Networked Multimedia Information System Laboratory, Italian National Research Council (2011)
12. Candela, L., Castelli, D., Pagano, P.: gcube v1.0: a software system for hybrid data infrastructures. Technical report 2008-TR-035, Istituto di Scienza e Tecnologie dell'Informazione "A. Faedo", CNR (2008)
13. Candela, L., Castelli, D., Pasquale, P.: Making virtual research environments in the cloud a reality: the gcube approach. ERCIM News **93**, 32–33 (2010). http://ercim-news.ercim.eu/en83/special/making-virtual-research-environments-in-the-cloud-a-reality-the-gcube-approach. Accessed 6 Jul 2016
14. Candela, L., Castelli, D., Pasquale, P.: gCube: a service-oriented application framework on the grid. ERCIM News **72**, 48–48 (2008). http://ercim-news.ercim.eu/en72/rd/gcube-a-service-oriented-application-framework-on-the-grid. Accessed 6 Jul 2016
15. Candelaa, L., Castellia, D., Manzib, A., Paganoa, P.: Realising virtual research environments by hybrid data infrastructures: the d4science experience. In: International Symposium on Grids and Clouds (ISGC), vol. 23 (2014)
16. Card, S.K., Mackinlay, J.D., Shneiderman, B. (eds.): Readings in Information Visualization: Using Vision to Think. Morgan Kaufmann Publishers Inc., San Francisco (1999)
17. Carp, J.: A web platform for streamlining scientific workflows, June 2014. https://opensource.com/life/14/6/center-open-science-framework. Accessed 5 Jul 2016
18. Carusi, A., Reimer, T.: Virtual Research Environment Collaborative Landscape Study, p. 106. JISC, Bristol (2010)
19. Center for Open Science: Open science framework (2011). https://osf.io/. Accessed 5 Jul 2016
20. Chang, R., Ziemkiewicz, C., Green, T., Ribarsky, W.: Defining insight for visual analytics. IEEE Comput. Graph. Appl. **29**(2), 14–17 (2009)
21. Consortium, D.: D4science (2016). https://www.d4science.org/. Accessed 6 Jul 2016
22. Costabile, M.F., Mussio, P., Parasiliti Provenza, L., Piccinno, A.: Supporting end users to be co-designers of their tools. In: Pipek, V., Rosson, M.B., Ruyter, B., Wulf, V. (eds.) IS-EUD 2009. LNCS, vol. 5435, pp. 70–85. Springer, Heidelberg (2009). doi:10.1007/978-3-642-00427-8_5
23. Davenport, T.H.: Analytics 3.0, December 2013. https://hbr.org/2013/12/analytics-30. Accessed 5 Jan 2016
24. EGI Foundation - EGI.eu: Egi federated cloud. https://www.egi.eu/infrastructure/cloud/. Accessed 10 Jan 2016
25. Fischer, G.: In defense of demassification: empowering individuals. Hum. Comput. Interact. **9**(1), 66–70 (1994)

26. Fischer, G., Nakakoji, K.: Beyond the macho approach of artificial intelligence: empower human designers - do not replace them. Knowl. Based Syst. **5**(1), 15–30 (1992)
27. Fischer, G.: Context-aware systems: The 'right' information, at the 'right' time, in the 'right' place, in the 'right' way, to the 'right' person. In: Proceedings of the International Working Conference on Advanced Visual Interfaces, AVI 2012, pp. 287–294. ACM, New York (2012)
28. Fraunhofer Institute for Computer Graphics Research IGD: Visual business analytics (2015). http://www.igd.fraunhofer.de/en/Institut/Abteilungen/ Informationsvisualisierung-und-Visual-Analytics/Visual-Business-Analytics. Accessed 2 Dec 2015
29. Freiknecht, J.: Big Data in der Praxis. Carl Hanser Verlag GmbH & Co. KG, München (2014)
30. Gartner, Inc.: Gartner it glossary knowledge management (km) (2013). http:// www.gartner.com/it-glossary/km-knowledge-management. Accessed 17 Nov 2015
31. gCube Consortium: gcube (version 1.5) (2016). https://www.gcube-system.org/. Accessed 6 Jul 2016
32. Hameed, I.: Knowledge management and business intelligence: what is the difference? (2004)
33. Helmholtz-Gemeinschaft: Definition: Virtual research environments, February 2011. http://www.allianzinitiative.de/en/core_activities/virtual_research_environm ents/definition/. Accessed 11 Jan 2016
34. Hemmje, M.L., Brocks, H., Becker, J. (eds.) Demand Of Data Science Skills & Competences (Expert Roundtable), November 2015
35. Herschel, R.T., Jones, N.E.: Knowledge management and business intelligence: the importance of integration. J. Knowl. Manage. **9**(4), 45–55 (2005)
36. Hoe, S.L.: Tacit knowledge, nonaka and takeuchi seci model and informal knowledge processes. Int. J. Organ. Theory Behav. **9**, 490–502 (2006)
37. Kaufmann, M.: Towards a reference model for big data management, research Report (2016, forthcoming)
38. Keim, D., Mansmann, F., Schneidewind, J., Ziegler, H.: Challenges in visual data analysis. In: Tenth International Conference on Information Visualization, IV 2006, pp. 9–16, July 2006
39. Keim, D.A., Mansmann, F., Thomas, J.: Visual analytics: How much visualization and how much analytics? SIGKDD Explor. Newsl. **11**(2), 5–8 (2010). http://doi.acm.org/10.1145/1809400.1809403
40. Kuhlen, R.: Informationsethik: Umgang mit Wissen und Information in elektronischen Räumen. UTB/UTB, UVK-Verlag-Ges (2004)
41. Markus, M.L., Majchrzak, A., Gasser, L.: A design theory for systems that support emergent knowledge processes. MIS Q. **26**(3), 179–212 (2002). http://dl.acm.org/citation.cfm?id=2017167.2017170
42. National Institute of Standards and Technology: The nist definition of cloud computing. Recommendations of the National Institute of Standards and Technology (2011). http://csrc.nist.gov/publications/nistpubs/800-145/Spp.800-145.pdf. Accessed 5 Jan 2016
43. Nonaka, I., Takeuchi, H.: The Knowledge-Creating Company: How Japanese Companies Create the Dynamics of Innovation. Oxford University Press, Oxford (1995)
44. Olson, B.: Differences between business intelligence and knowledge management, February 2014. http://theitprofessor.blogspot.de/2014/02/differences-between-business.html. Accessed 16 Nov 2015

45. Ozsu, M.T.: Principles of Distributed Database Systems, 2nd edn. Prentice Hall Press, Upper Saddle River (1999)
46. Palace, B.: Data mining: What is data mining? Anderson Graduate School of Management, University of California, Los Angeles, June 1996
47. Patel, N.V., Ghoneim, A.: Managing emergent knowledge through deferred action design principles: the case of ecommerce virtual teams (2011)
48. Python Software Foundation: Python community (1991). https://www.python.org/community/. Accessed 5 Jul 2016
49. van Rijmenam, M.: Business intelligence vs. business analytics: What's the difference? November 2014
50. Saggion, H., Funk, A., Maynard, D., Bontcheva, K.: Ontology-based information extraction for business intelligence. In: Aberer, K., et al. (eds.) ASWC/ISWC - 2007. LNCS, vol. 4825, pp. 843–856. Springer, Heidelberg (2007). doi:10.1007/978-3-540-76298-0_61
51. Shi, G.: Data integration using agent based mediator-wrapper architecture. Technical report, Department of Electrical and Computer Engineering, The University of Calgary (2002)
52. Shneiderman, B.: The eyes have it: a task by data type taxonomy for information visualizations. In: IEEE Symposium on Visual Languages, 1996, Proceedings, pp. 336–343, September 1996
53. Singh, D., Reddy, C.K.: A survey on platforms for big data analytics. J. Big Data 2(1), 1–20 (2014). http://dx.doi.org/10.1186/s40537-014-0008-6
54. Thomas, J.J., Cook, K., et al.: A visual analytics agenda. IEEE Comput. Graph. Appl. 26(1), 10–13 (2006)
55. Thomas, J.J., Cook, K.A.: Illuminating the Path: The Research and Development Agenda for Visual Analytics. National Visualization and Analytics Center, Richland (2005)
56. Upadhyay, S., Grant, R.: 5 data scientists who became ceos and are leading thriving companies, October 2013. http://venturebeat.com/2013/12/03/5-data-scientists-who-became-ceos-and-are-leading-thriving-companies/. Accessed 30 Oct 2015
57. Wiederhold, G.: Mediators in the architecture of future information systems. Computer 25(3), 38–49 (1992)
58. Wong, P.C., Thomas, J.: Visual analytics. IEEE Comput. Graph. Appl. 5, 20–21 (2004)

Engineering Study of Tidal Stream Renewable Energy Generation and Visualization: Issues of Process Modelling and Implementation

John Harrison[1] and James Uhomobhi[2(✉)]

[1] School of Engineering, Ulster University, Belfast, Northern Ireland, UK
Harrison-J2@email.ulster.ac.uk
[2] Faculty of Computing and Engineering, Computer Science Research Institute (CSRI),
Ulster University, Belfast, Northern Ireland, UK
j.uhomoibhi@ulster.ac.uk

Abstract. Tidal stream energy has the potential to make a significant contribution to energy mix in the future. Accurate modelling and visualisation of both tidal resource and array layout enhances understanding of in-stream tidal behaviour leading to improvements in site identification and optimal positioning of individual turbines. A realistic representation of blade loading conditions will aid designers and manufacturers in creating more robust devices and improve survivability. The main barriers to large scale deployments of tidal arrays are the costs associated with manufacturing, installation and maintenance. Therefore, presently tidal energy is not competitive on cost with more established renewable technologies. The current position paper investigates and reports on resource modelling, site selection, selecting optimal array configurations and the design and manufacture of devices for tidal stream renewable energy generation. This is aimed at developing models to reliably simulate real conditions, enhance understanding of tidal processes, flow regimes and device survivability issues.

Keywords: Tidal stream energy · Tidal turbines · Tidal resource · Visualisation · Modelling

1 Introduction

Renewable energy generation is growing in relevance due to the dual issues of continuing global warming and national security of electrical supply. A largely untapped potential resource is ocean energy which has the global potential to supply 170 TW of electricity annually [1]. Of the currently available technologies to extract energy from the oceans only tidal range, which takes advantage of the vertical height difference between high and low tide, is at a mature stage of development [2]. A nascent alternative tidal technology exists which seeks to exploit horizontal fluid motion and is less intrusive than tidal range installations [3], in stream tidal turbines, and operates using the same basic principle as a wind turbine using seawater as the operating fluid rather than wind [4].

© Springer International Publishing AG 2016
M.X. Bornschlegl et al. (Eds.): AVI-BDA 2016, LNCS 10084, pp. 19–34, 2016.
DOI: 10.1007/978-3-319-50070-6_2

Tidal science is a developed field of study and the predictable nature of tidal motions overcomes stochastic issues faced by other renewable technologies, most notably wind and wave [5]. Predictability provides an advantage not only for grid management but also for accurate financial forecasting which is a key obstacle to the widespread installation of tidal stream turbine arrays [1]. Within the UK there is a desire to progress deployment of tidal stream technology and the Crown Estate, responsible for the seabed around the UK, has leased 26 zones suitable for tidal stream arrays. If these projects are all realised, installed tidal stream capacity in the UK could reach 1200 MW [6].

Wave and tidal technologies are expected to make considerable contributions to the future of global electricity generation [5]. Ocean wave energy, much like wind energy, is stochastic in nature. The study of tidal flow is an established science and the effects of the Moon and Sun are well understood allowing accurate tidal forecasts [3, 5]. It has been argued [7, 8] that for this reason tidal energy is more reliable than other offshore energy sources. Also, the predictability of tidal energy provides an advantage for grid management as tidal output can be integrated more easily due to accurate forecasting. The sustainable integration of tidal energy as a major contributor to the renewable mix would require the development of devices which can operate in deep water (>50 m) and can extract energy from slower moving currents (<2 m/s) than currently possible, this will enable deployment a much greater area and reduce competition amongst developers for the most attractive sites.

The forecast is that early that early deployment of tidal stream turbines will lead to competitiveness being reached sooner and this is important to reduce the relative importance of fossil fuels. It is important therefore that industry should prioritise R&D to improve device efficiency rather than focusing on the identification of cost cutting measures. They also promote the development of energy storage techniques and smart grid networks which will aid the increased penetration of all intermittent renewable energy.

2   Tidal Range Technology and Science

In-stream tidal devices are designed to capture the horizontal motion of the tide, tidal range technology exploits the vertical motion of the tidal cycle. A dam is constructed across a bay or estuary which experiences a large tidal range (>5 m). Sluice gates at the dam base control fluid flow; these are kept closed until a sufficient head is built up across the dam wall. The gates are opened and water flows from the high side to the low side and in doing so passes through turbines which spin to produce electricity. Power is generated following both the flood and ebb tides with the high water being on the ocean side of the dam during flood tides and water being held within the bay during the ebb tide [3]. Variations on the scheme include tidal lagoons, reefs and tidal fences, all of which operates using the same principle.

The most established tidal range plant is La Rance in France which has been in operation since 1967 and generates 480 GW hrs per year. A 720 m long barrage separates the river estuary from the ocean and twenty-four 10 MW reversible turbines are installed along its length. The power plant combines two-way operation with pumped storage to act as a reserve [2, 3]. The basin captures a 22 km^2 water area with the dam doubling as a road link and the installation has become a popular tourist attraction.

2.1 Tidal Levels and Parameter Descriptions

The regular rise and fall of the water level of the ocean is principally caused by gravitational and centrifugal forces which are a result of the proximity of the Earth to the Moon and the Sun [3]. When the water flows towards the shore it is called a flood tide while the receding water is called the ebb tide. This occurs on at least a diurnal (daily) basis in all areas of the world and for coastal areas in northwest Europe the tide exhibits strongly semi-diurnal (twice daily) behaviour [3, 9].

High tide on earth occurs "in line" with the Moon and conversely low tide is + experienced at +/−90° relative to the Moon. A second major influence is that of the Sun, because the Sun is much further from Earth the gravitational force it exerts is around 0.45 that of the Moon. When the Earth, Moon and Sun system is in alignment the gravitational effects of the Moon and Sun are combined to form a high tidal range (a spring tide), when the Moon and Sun are at 90° to one another, as viewed from Earth, the gravitational effects of the Moon are counteracted by those from the Sun, leading to an exceptionally low tidal range (a neap tide) [3].

The velocity at which the tidal water flows varies from zero m/s at periods of slack water to a maximum value which occurs halfway between periods of slack water [3]. A mathematical description of the tide is that it exhibits a sinusoidal behaviour and is made up of a number of harmonics each with a varying degree of influence. The principle influences of the Moon (M2 – lunar semi-diurnal) which has a period of 12.42 h and Sun (S2 – solar semi-diurnal) which has a period of exactly 12 h are the largest constituents. The tide is also affected by local bathymetry, ocean currents, weather and density gradients. The period of M2 results in high tide occurring approximately 50 min later each day [9]. The relationship between the M2 and S2 constituents means that a spring – neap cycle lasts approximately 14.75 days. Tidal asymmetry is a result of the influence of M4 (lunar quarter-diurnal) constituent which is largely a consequence of local bathymetry [9]. The relationship between the phases of M2 and M4 could potentially lead to a tidal resource only providing maximum output for one cycle per day even in a strongly semi-diurnal region.

2.2 The Cost of Ocean Energy

Cost is seen as a major barrier to the wide scale deployment of ocean energy technology [10]. In order to improve investor confidence accurate resource assessment and forecasting models are required [6] (Fig. 1).

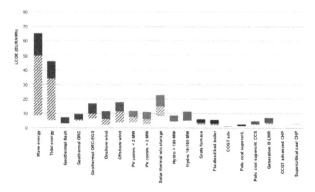

Fig. 1. Cost of Ocean Energy (Blue LHS of chart) vs other forms of electricity generation [11]

Cost reduction should be a target for the in stream tidal energy industry and reliable visual models for resource assessment and assessing the impact of turbine arrays on flow regimes should be developed. These could help to eliminate the current dependence on costly and time consuming empirical data collection. There is also a need to improve device manufacturing techniques, accurate modelling of blade loading conditions will expedite blade and tower design consensus thus enabling greater supply chain competition. While models which accurately portray the cyclic nature of tidal loading will help to improve design for survivability and improve understanding regarding the detrimental effects of seawater ingress, particularly when designing with composite materials.

3   Technology Design and Implementation

There are three main types of devices for capturing the energy contained in tidal streams. They include (i) horizontal axis tidal turbine, (ii) vertical axis tidal turbine and (iii) reciprocating or hydrofoil devices [3]. Each of the designs attempt to extract the kinetic energy contained in the tidal and convert this to rotational motion via rotor blades which in turn produces electricity from a generator.

Devices which are installed at greater depths can have larger sweet areas and therefore capture more tidal energy. However this comes with greater installation costs [8]. The principle of operation is similar to that of a wind turbine. Seawater is much denser than air and typically travels at lower speed. The turbine must generate electricity during both flood and ebb tides and be capable of withstanding structural loads [3]. The tidal turbine blades are of a hydrofoil design. This facilitates the extraction of energy from fluid flow.

3.1   Current Guidelines

In general, the most promising areas are found in ocean channels or straights where tidal flow is forced through a narrow cross section e.g. the Pentland Firth (Scotland) or Alderney (English Channel). Using Fig. 2. [12] it is possible to identify those sites around the UK where tidal flow velocities are greatest, these are the most attractive sites for development. There is also a challenge when classifying the tidal velocity at a particular site as velocities will vary within the water column and across the cross section due to local bathymetry [13], therefore an average velocity is not sufficiently accurate to allow a developer to position turbines. For the reasons outlined above the European Marine Energy Centre (EMEC) have produced guidelines for resource assessment which recommend a developer conduct extensive onsite measurements when identifying a potential tidal site [14].

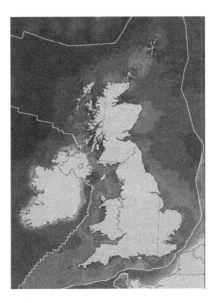

Fig. 2. Peak Flow for a Mean Spring Tide (areas in yellow have high velocity flow i.e. >2 m/s) (Color figure online)

A challenge posed by the approach of EMEC is the time consuming and expensive installation of measurement apparatus. The development of advanced models to quickly and accurately predict tidal flows will benefit both site developers and academics by allowing the analysis of a greater number of potential sites without the need for extensive onsite measurements.

Velocity is of interest because the power output of a tidal turbine is related to the cube of water velocity, the power available at the rotor is found from,

$$P_t = \frac{\rho \cdot A_r \cdot v^3}{2} \tag{1}$$

Where P_t is the power available at the turbine rotor (W), ρ is the density of seawater (kg/m^3), A_r is the swept area of the rotor blades (m^2) and v^3 is the velocity of the seawater (m/s) passing through A_r.

There are a number of observers who highlight that looking purely at maximum flow velocities during the site selection process is superficial [15], these authors encourage a leasing strategy which reflects the need for phase diversity between tidal sites in order to provide a firm supply of electrical energy onto the national grid.

3.2 Blades Variation and Energy Capture

Tidal turbine blades are of a hydrofoil design in order to extract energy from a fluid flow. This is similar to the working principle of a wind turbine but with tidal stream devices the ratio between the density of the fluid and the blade's material is much closer to 1 [16]. For purposes of comparison, loads experienced by a tidal turbine's blade is much greater than those experienced by a wind turbine blade. There is the need for greater under-standing of the loads faced by blades as unsteady loading may exceed steady state loading by up to 15% during a tidal cycle. Not all the power available to the turbine can be converted into electricity. The power equation must be adapted to reflect device efficiency. This is done with the inclusion of a capacity factor (C_p) into Eq. 1 as an expression for electrical power (P_E), given by:

$$P_E = C_p \frac{\rho * A * v^3}{2} \tag{2}$$

For present technology, a value of 0.35 has been suggested as a reasonable value for C_p, measured value of 0.285 has been reported [17, 18] and very recently when conducting field measurements of a full scale (50 kW) horizontal axis turbine at Strang-ford Lough, a maximum Cp value of 0.35 has been recorded [19]. Design stability is a crucial step for development of supply chains and the reduction of costs associated with manufacturing.

Visualisation is important at all stages of design. Industry must define clear guide-lines on survivability and reliability requirements by implementing universal standards for designers and manufacturers to meet This leads to enhanced cooperation amongst stakeholders [1, 20]. Horizontal axis tidal turbines have been shown to be the most developed and proven technology. Over 76% of global research and development investment in tidal technology has been dedicated to developing horizontal axis devices [20]. This is also the most extensively proven technology with devices connected to the UK grid over the most recent period of six years.

There are two variations of the horizontal axis design. They include (i) devices which have a yawing mechanism enabling them to face into the direction of the tidal current and (ii) devices where the blades are placed on one side of the supporting structure and rotate through 180 degrees to extract energy from both sides [21]. Studies undertaken with the former have shown tower structures always interfere with fluid flow. Placing the rotor downstream during either flood or ebb tends to pose a significant issue due to blades passing through the sheltered area. This is minimized by increasing the clearance distance between rotor blades and the tower. Studies of the effects of loading two, three and four blade horizontal axis turbine models have been reported [22] and they suggest possible methods to improve energy extraction before the blade reaches its optimal setting.

4   Resource Assessment and Modelling

A two stage approach has been suggested for when analysing a site's potential as tidal resource [9]. Initially only the M2 and S2 constituent harmonics are considered to establish the character of a site. This is followed by the next step which is one of developing the model to include the effects M4 and the other lesser tidal harmonics. The European Marine Energy Centre (EMEC), have published guidelines for tidal site developers in which they advocate the use of extensive onsite measurements as part of a resource assessment [23]. The challenge this poses is that the offshore deployment of measurement apparatus is a costly and time consuming endeavour. Another technique involves the use of two methods which utilise recorded current speeds, at a known vertical distance from the seabed, to estimate flow in the water column. The Van Veen and von Karman approaches each use a dimensionless factor, found from experiment, to extrapolate a known tidal stream velocity to any desired height in the water column. The availability of accurate tidal stream charts in some regions offer the prospect of using known surface currents to extrapolate to depths where turbines are located.

4.1   Site Location and Description

The north coast of Antrim is an area with a high velocity flow regime. Alternative methods to investigate resource availability are explored in this paper. We attempt establishing the velocity profile without the need for extensive field studies by using existing publications and data to conduct resource assessments. In this paper we relied on known surface currents to estimate flow regime in the water column and utilised tidal range over a known area to calculate volumetric flow, which can then be simulated using a computational fluid dynamics (CFD) model. Regional flow regimes during flood tides are a result of underwater features and the Rathlin Island headland. These divide water flowing from the ocean with a disproportionate volume flowing through an area off the north Antrim coast. High velocity ebb tides are a consequence of flow direction with most of the fluid volume exiting the Irish Sea through the northern channel originating from the region of tidal resonance to the west of England. A comparison is then made with flow through a bend in a pipe, where the external radius witnesses a higher flow regime than the internal radius.

4.2   Methodology and Use of Surface Flow Charts

Published tidal stream charts for the northern channel are available at: http://www.visit-myharbour.com/articles/3166/hourly-tidal-streams-around-the-n-of-ireland-and-sw-of-scotland. The charts are produced for recreational sea users such as light sailing and kayaking. The charts show flow magnitude and direction at 13 hourly intervals. Time is referenced from six hours before high water at a regional control port to six hours after high tide, for UK and Irish waters the control port is Dover (England). The surface velocities are presented as maximum and minimum values, to correspond with spring and neap tides, all other velocities are assumed to fall within these boundaries.

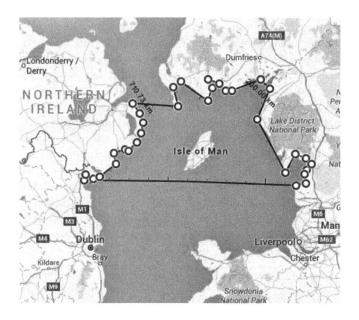

Fig. 3. Area of Irish Sea filled from the Northern Channel

The present study area is shown outlined in black in Fig. 3. It encompasses a total area of 13,540 Km^2 with a water area of approximately 12,990 km^2. There are eight zones with differing tidal range within this area.

Another method used to estimate the velocity profile at a site was to use knowledge of tidal range over a known area to calculate the volume of fluid flow during the tidal cycle. Tide tables are available for ports around the world and have been calculated by recording tidal range over a long period and combining the constituent harmonics to extrapolate forward. Tidal range data is widely and freely available in the form of tide tables. The National Tide and Sea Level Facility (NTSLF) record live data for tidal range at selected ports around the UK and these are accessible online at http://www.ntslf.org/data/uk-network-real-time. Live data can be compared with tide table to validate the accuracy of tidal range forecasts. Tidal data for February 2016 has been used to analyse the resource potential of a site located in the Northern Channel which connects the Irish Sea with the North Atlantic Ocean. The Irish Sea (Fig. 4 red box) is a body of water separating Ireland from Britain which is connected to the North Atlantic Ocean by channels to the north and south. Tide tables are available for ports in this region, tidal stream charts are also available for both the flood and ebb tides. The tide is funnelled through a narrow cross section just off the coast of north Antrim (Fig. 4 blue box) as a result this area shows promise as a potential high energy tidal site.

Fig. 4. Irish Sea Showing points of interest in understanding tidal behaviour (NTSLF.org, 2016) (Color figure online)

In order to characterise tidal flow in the area of interest it is first necessary to develop an understanding of the behaviour of the tidal regime in the region. It is established that north western European shelf seas are strongly semidiurnal and this is confirmed by the tide tables for the region. As a result of the tidal regime in the Irish Sea there are four points of interest during the fortnightly tidal cycle. They include the Spring high tide, the Spring low tide, the Neap high tide and the Neap low tide. Analysis of the data shows that high water occurs at similar times at all ports within the Irish Sea's main body of water. This posed the difficulty associated with estimating volume flow through each channel based on the timing of high and low tide at various ports.

4.3 Tidal Range Data and Tidal Charts

In order to develop the required models, without using onsite measurements, available tidal range data and published surface tidal velocity charts should be exploited. Studies have been conducted [24], which seek to determine flow velocity using conservation of mass methods. The principle is, the tidal volume which flows into a body of water must have come through a channel which connects that body with the ocean.

A review of tidal charts reveals that the Irish Sea fills from both the north and south simultaneously, therefore the total height gained, as measured by onshore tidal range monitors, must have entered from these two channels (high tide). The tide then exits simultaneously through the same two channels resulting in a lower sea level (low tide). This cycle of high and low tide is repeated twice every day due to strongly semidiurnal tidal behaviour in the region with maximum (spring) and minimum (neap) tides occurring on a biweekly cycle (Fig. 5).

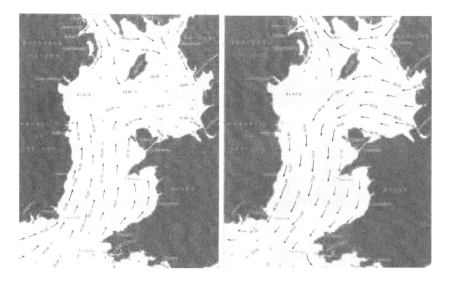

Fig. 5. Flood & Ebb Tides in Irish Sea (source: http://www.visitmyharbour.com, 2016)

The ability to accurately visualise this flow enables a greater understanding of tidal behaviour and of the mathematics required to describe it. Both tidal range and tidal flow exhibit sinusoidal behaviour, as a result the volume of water which flows during a tidal cycle ranges from a maximum value at peak flow to zero during periods of slack water. In order to describe something which changes over time differential calculus is the most appropriate tool. Vennell developed the relationship:

$$A_B * \frac{dh}{dt} = Q$$

Where Q is the volumetric flow (m^3/s) required to rise the water level by h (m) in the body of water AB (m2). This simple relationship can be used to calculate volumetric flow through a channel which connects an enclosed body of water with the ocean and was developed to analyse a Norwegian Fjord.

To accurately model tidal flow, once volumetric flow is known, requires only accurate information regarding channel bathymetry and seafloor composition. NASA's satellites have accurately measured the earth's surface and ocean contours with the files being publicly available and coefficient of friction is known for many seafloor types. It can only be a matter of time before models of tidal flow are developed which are sufficiently accurate to eliminate the current need for extensive onsite data collection.

5 Array Layout

In order to maximise the potential of high energy tidal sites it is likely that turbines will be grouped together into arrays, much in the same way wind turbines are often grouped together to form wind farms. Tidal arrays will face challenges due to their harsh operating environment and the loads created by a dense operating fluid. The following must be taken into consideration in an array layout:

5.1 Wake Interactions

Visual models which show wake interactions will be of great importance to tidal site developers as the available resource at each turbine can be significantly affected by any upstream turbines [9]. The effect is not always negative and studies suggest it is possible to exceed the Betz limit when siting a turbine within a tidal array due to the venturi effect of funnelling water between turbines [17], and while this could lead to greater output it will also lead to greater loads being experienced at the rotor blades. Any induced wake effect will be a compromise between maximum output and device survivability.

5.2 Blade Behaviour

Due to the significant loads created by seawater, blade designs and manufacturing methods will be a crucial aspect of maintaining device performance during operation. Fluctuations in water velocity create much greater loads than those experienced in wind turbines. In order to prevent damage to blades it is important to develop increased understanding of blade deformation and vibration in order to improve modelling and simulation leading to improved blade designs. Current studies are considering whether to allow turbine blades to flex under stress before reaching their optimal design [20] such research exposes the high level of concern over loading conditions for turbines placed in the open ocean. An accurate model which can visually represent realistic conditions at sea would be invaluable for design and R&D practitioners, and would permit reliable simulations which are much less costly and time consuming than sea trials or other physical testing regimes.

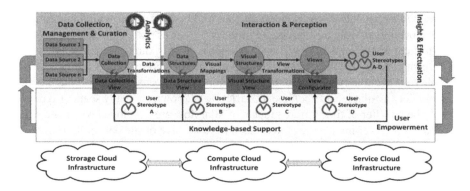

Fig. 6. The IVIS4BigData Reference model. Source: Bornschlegl, et al. (2016) [25]

5.3 Sediment Transport

A potential adverse environmental impact of installing a tidal array is the effect on local sediment transport due to a reduction in flow velocity. Modelling work has been conducted in the Pentland Firth where a number of tidal arrays are planned to be installed. A major challenge when investigating the possible localised impacts of a tidal array is a lack of commercial scale developments and at present there are no sizable tidal stream installations anywhere in the world, as a result it is likely that the first sites to be developed will be monitored extensively to ascertain environmental impacts.

It is difficult at present to imagine a model which could accurately simulate all environmental effects of reduced tidal flow and channel blockage, however a visual model to predict regular issues such as sediment transport or more stochastic events, that is, marine megafauna interaction may be possible in the future with more practical experience and monitoring of tidal stream arrays.

6   Results, Visualisation and Discussion

6.1 Visualization and the IVIS4BigData Reference Model

The IVIS4BigData reference model [25] applied to our current work provides a framework consisting of interlinked set of clearly defined concepts in the generation and visualization of tidal stream renewable energy for improved modelling and implementation. It helps clarify issues and promote clear communication in relation to design, development and implementation. The present research involves the collection, management and curation of data drawn from a range of sources, some of which include EMEC (European Marine Energy Centre), tidal stream charts published online and reports issued by UK and Irish Waters control port in the UK. Some of the other sources also include the live data and those generated using algorithms developed with computer programs as programs Python, Java (Fig. 6).

Analysis systems (Matlab® and Mathematica™) are used for data transformation. 2D and 3D plots from tables of data generated are then utilised for visualisation of information for the provision of knowledge-based support for the various categories of users enabling and empowering development and deployment of services for the public, business and community sectors. In the world of tidal stream renewable energy generation and visualization, the IVIS4BigData reference model seems to help provides means of developing useful models that serve to create standards, educate, improve communication, create clear roles and responsibilities for all those involved. It also allows comparison between developments in different systems and practices.

6.2   Results Analysis and Discussions

Maximum daily tidal flows occur between 3–4 h before and after high water, approximately 25% of all flow is accounted for during one hour of the cycle. The total mass displaced was multiplied by 25% to model the flow during this period. An accurate representation of bathymetry is required to simulate flow through the northern channel. There are a number of sources of data which provide latitude and longitude co-ordinates and water depth. Google Earth is one of the possible sources of information. NASA's Radar Shuttle Topography Mission (RSTM) and the European Marine Observation and Data Network (EMODnet) offer reliable bathemetry data files available for download and use. These files are in various sformats (.asc,.emo,.mnt,.sd,.xyz,.hdr,.tfw,.prj). Manually sampled water depth obtained from the EMODnet's site over an approximate 80 km × 60 km grid from 55.00 to 55.75 Northings and from −5.50 to −6.50 Eastings, as a Matlab plot is shown in Fig. 7. Other available software applications can used, they include ANSYS, Solid Edge etc.

The magnitude of the tide is realistic with the model predicting a maximum neap flow velocity of 1.17 m/s. This numerical value is the correct order of magnitude and shows there is at least some potential to the method. Accurate bathymetry for a large distance upstream is a necessary model parameter. Modelling the ebb tide proved more successful as this is not heavily influenced by upstream bathymetry but by the positions of the large landmasses which were more easily represented when creating model geometry. The volumetric and mass flow rates calculated produce velocity estimates which were in the correct order of magnitude producing reasonable representations of realistic conditions during tidal cycle.

7   Conclusion

The ability to generate 3D models, which accurately reflect real world behaviour, is of great interest to practitioners in tidal stream energy. Visualisation of flow regimes will aid understanding of tidal flow allowing academics and students to better understand and describe behaviour, while this will also assist site developers who can assess a greater number of sites without the need for extensive onsite monitoring as is presently required.

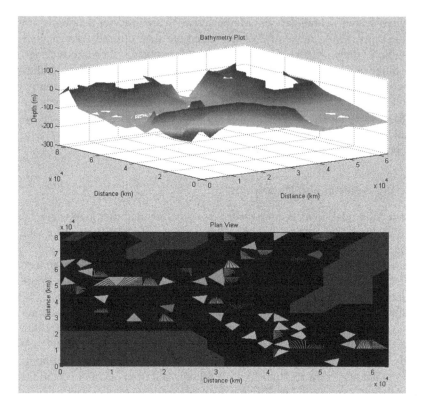

Fig. 7. Matlab plot of bathymetry data sample.

One of the benefits of an accurate resource modelling technique based on volume flow is that it allows more sites to be evaluated at less cost and greater speed. Volume flow can be calculated even in complex tidal regions. This has been demonstrated in the case of the northern Irish Sea. However, the method is believed would be best applied in a region with only one connecting channel with the ocean.

Those designing major components will benefit from models which can show blade and support structure loading conditions, allowing for design and reliable simulations without extensive physical validation which is both costly and time consuming. Site developers will be able to model many alternative array configurations using realistic and robust CFD models to establish optimal array configuration at each specific site. This will be a compromise between maximum efficiency of each individual turbine versus the output from the entire array and the acceptable in service loading on turbines. Although performance sensitivity is low for all turbine designs tested to date, the magnitude of deflection are found to be significantly influenced by pitch angle of the blade. Further studies and modelling are needed to establish whether blades should be intentionally designed to flex under loading before reaching their optimal configuration with consideration also being given to tower-rotor interactions and the effect of small perturbations, that is, deviations from regular state, on fatigue life [16].

In the future both academia and industry will benefit from robust, reliable models which accurately map out a 3D environment representing a potential tidal stream site. Greater understanding of the practicalities will lead to innovative solutions to challenges presented by the harsh operating environment and allow divergence of design for turbines and major subcomponents, leading to a competitive supply chain. The ultimate goal is to reduce costs and enable tidal stream turbines to become cost competitive with other forms of energy. If this is achieved the predictable behaviour of the tides can be exploited and managed to produce vast quantities of firm electrical energy onto the UK national grid over the coming years.

References

1. Sgobbi, A., Simoes, S., Magagna, D., Nijs, W.: Assessing the impacts of technology improvements on the deployment of marine energy in Europe with an energy system perspective. Renew. Energy **89**, 515–525 (2016)
2. Waters, S., Aggidis, G.: Tidal range technologies and state of the art in review. Renew. Sustain. Energy Rev. **59**, 514–529 (2016)
3. O'Rourke, F., Boyle, F., Reynolds, A.: Tidal energy update 2009. Appl. Energy **87**, 398–409 (2010)
4. Cengel, Y., Turner, R., Cimbala, J.: Fundamentals of Thermal-Fluid Sciences Third Edition in SI Units, 3rd edn. McGraw Hill, Singapore (2008)
5. Uihlein, A., Magagna, D.: Wave and tidal current energy – a review of the current state of research beyond technology. Renew. Sustain. Energy Rev. **58**, 1070–1081 (2016)
6. BERR (Department for Business, Enterprise & Regulatory Reform). Atlas of UK Marine Renewable Energy Resources. London: APBmer, The Met Office, Proudman Oceanographic Laboratory (2008)
7. Funke, S., Farrell, P., Piggott, M.: Tidal turbine array optimisation using the adjoint approach. Renew. Energy **63**, 658–673 (2014)
8. Lewis, M., Neill, S., Robins, P., Hashemi, M.: Resource assessment for future generations of tidal-stream energy arrays. Energy **83**, 403–415 (2015)
9. Robins, P., Neill, S., Lewis, M., Ward, S.: Characterising the spatial and temporal variability of the tidal-stream energy resource over the northwest European shelf seas. Appl. Energy **147**, 510–522 (2015)
10. Lalander, E., Thomassen, P., Leijon, M.: Evaluation of a model for predicting the tidal velocity in fjord entrances. Energies **6**, 2031–2051 (2013)
11. Vennell, R.: Estimating the power potential of tidal currents and the impact of power extraction on flow speeds. Renew. Energy **36**, 3558–3565 (2011)
12. visitmyharbour.com. Tidal Charts for Spring and Neap tides (2015). http://www.visitmyharbour.com/tides/. Accessed 1 Jul 2016
13. Hardisty, J.: The Analysis of Tidal Stream Power. Wiley, Chichester (2009)
14. Nasa.gov, NASA Jet Propulsion Laboratory - Shuttle Radar Topography Mission SRTM. http://srtm.usgs.gov/index.php
15. Kolliatsas, C., Dudziak, G., Schaefer, J., Myers, N.: Offshore Renewable Energy: Accelerating the Deployment of Offshore Wind, Tidal and Wave Technologies. Earthscan, New York (2012)
16. Milne, I., Day, A., Sharma, R., Flay, R.: Blade loading on tidal turbines for uniform unsteady flow. Renew. Energy **77**, 338–350 (2015)

17. Neill, S., Hashemi, M., Lewis, M.: Tidal energy leasing and tidal phasing. Renew. Energy **85**, 580–597 (2016)
18. Doman, D., Murray, R., Pegg, M., Gracie, K., Johnstone, C., Nevalainen, T.: Tow-tank testing of a 1/20th scale horizontal axis tidal turbine with uncertainty analysis. Int. J. Mar. Energy **11**, 105–119 (2015)
19. Jeffcoate, P., Starzmann, R., Elsaesser, B., Scholl, S., Bischoff, S.: Field measurements of a full scale tidal turbine. Int. J. Mar. Energy **12**, 3–20 (2015)
20. Magagna, D., Uihlein, A.: Ocean energy development in Europe: current status and future perspectives. Int. J. Mar. Energy **11**, 84–104 (2015)
21. Frost, C., Morris, C., Mason-Jones, A., O'Doherty, D., O'Doherty, T.: The effect of tidal flow directionality on tidal turbine performance characteristics. Renew. Energy **78**, 609–620 (2015)
22. Morris, C., O'Doherty, D., O'Doherty, T., Mason-Jones, A.: Kinetic energy extraction of a tidal stream turbine and its sensitivity to structural stiffness attenuation. Renew. Energy **88**, 30–39 (2016)
23. European Marine Energy Centre: Assessment of Tidal Energy Resource – Marine Renewable Energy Guides. The Charlesworth Group, London (2009)
24. Fairley, I., Masters, I., Karunarathna, H.: The cumulative impact of tidal stream turbine arrays on sediment transport in the Pentland Firth. Renew. Energy **80**, 755–769 (2015)
25. Bornschlegl, M.X., Berwind, K., Kaufmann, M., Engel, F.C., Walsh, P., Hemmje, M.L., Riestra, R., Werkmann, B.: IVIS4BigData: A Reference Model for Advanced Visual Interfaces Supporting Big Data Analysis in Virtual Research Environments (2016). https://www.researchgate.net/publication/306038480_Towards_a_Reference_Model_for_Advanced_Visual_Interfaces_Supporting_Big_Data_Analysis and http://www.lgmmia.fernuni-hagen.de/bib/docs/Bor_16b.html.en. Accessed 6 Sep 2016

Cost Effective Visualization of Research Data for Cognitive Development Using Mobile Augmented Reality

Clement Onime[1] and James Uhomobhi[2(✉)]

[1] The Abdus Salam International Centre for Theoretical Physics, Trieste, Italy
onime@ictp.it
[2] Ulster University, Belfast, Northern Ireland
j.uhomoibhi@ulster.ac.uk

Abstract. In many fields of science, the numerical output of research work require proper interpretation in relation to real world situations. Graphical visualization is often used to ensure better comprehension of data (research outputs) by researchers, learners and other stakeholders. However, in the modern era, large scale experimentation as well as computer-based simulations are generating massive amounts of numeric data that are almost impossible to visualize using traditional plots and graphs as they are limited in both dimensions and scale. Video has gained increasing popularity for presenting data due to its ability to convey motion and time. While, such video presentations are undoubtedly useful, they provide limited contributions to cognitive development. In this paper, we examine a cost effective use of mobile Augmented Reality (AR) in the visualization of scientific research data highlighting two use-cases that show the Three Dimensional (3D) semi-immersive and interactive environment in both educational and non-educational contexts.

Keywords: mobile Augmented Reality · Computer assisted instruction

1 Introduction

Computers and other Information and Communication Technology (ICT) tools present information (data) using different media types and formats such as text, graphics, video and animations. For example, a simple hand-held computer device could present alphanumeric text such as the American Standard Code for Information Interchange (ASCII) characters on a monochromatic Liquid Crystal Display (LCD) digital display, while, the Personal Computer (PC) has evolved over the last three decades in their ability to present information in multimedia, that is using a mix of computer generated characters, graphics, animations or digital video, all on a color visual display unit.

Figure 1 provide a visual comparison of the information carrying ability of different forms of (electronic) formats/media commonly used by computers and ICT tools in presenting data. The "text and document" formats at the bottom of the pyramid (Fig. 1) employs significantly more symbols in conveying the same amount of information as a graphical plot (image) and many images are needed to convey the same information as a video animation. In practical terms, Fig. 1 implies that it requires significantly larger

© Springer International Publishing AG 2016
M.X. Bornschlegl et al. (Eds.): AVI-BDA 2016, LNCS 10084, pp. 35–49, 2016.
DOI: 10.1007/978-3-319-50070-6_3

amount of text and graphs/plots to show (replicate) the volume of time-dependent data presented in an animation or audio/video fragment/clip. This is supported by the current trend in online/distance learning, where Massive Open On-line Course (MOOC) platforms favor the use of audio/visual clips and animations over traditional textual/image presentations for the delivery of knowledge (or voluminous information) to a vast audience of learners.

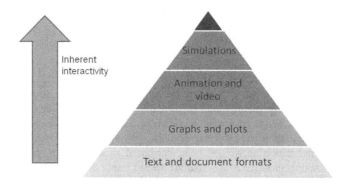

Fig. 1. Information and digital-format relationship diagram [30].

Researchers regularly employ computers and ICT tools in the acquisition, storage, processing and presentation of data [10, 12]. For example, data about real world events may be digitized by appropriate sensors during acquisition and stored on suitable media such as magnetic or optical media or other solid-state devices. A suitable computer application is then used to process data and perform functionalities such as checking for accuracy and also quantitative or qualitative analysis. During this stage, the data may be described, summarized (or reduced), compared to other datasets and/or prepared for interpretation. Subsequently, the processed data may be represented in one or more suitable formats for presentation. For example, tables or descriptive text be used may provide summary information about data, graphical representations are useful in providing an overview, while animations and videos are especially suited to conveying additional information such as motion, progress or movement. In this position paper, we use the term "research data" to describe the outputs obtained from a scientific investigation process.

General cognitive improvements may be derived from external stimuli such as drinking caffeinated beverages, the use of prescription medication or other suitable operant conditioning [41]. The disposition of a learner to learning which is distinct from his/her individual learning style is fundamental for cognitive development and even when teaching styles such as classroom/tutorials practised at institutions of higher education do not match the learning styles, introducing multimedia content into a course can produce measurable improvements in learning [43]. In most academic institutions, transfer of knowledge and cognitive development, that is encouraging intellectual reasoning and creating knowledge or know-how occurs within preset environments such as a classroom for face-to-face teaching/learning or on-line learning platforms. Sometimes, during class-room lessons, the display of video or animation are included as part of some active learning processes, while the earlier mentioned MOOCs and other on-line environments simulate cognitive development in both non-formal and formal learning context. Indeed, when learning with objects such as research data, the academic reasoning process is highly simulated by interactivity such as human-to-human [23] communication and/or other forms of interactivity [30]. It may be said that the contributions to cognitive development become significantly enhanced when learning objects such as research data are presented/studied with interactivity.

Researchers are increasingly tasked with studying and understanding systems with increased complexities or sometimes in dimensions (scales) that are difficult to achieve experimentally. Often, the solution is the use of simulations that allows them to explore in details the item or situation under study. Within a simulation, the researcher can quickly effect variations and with minimum delay, obtain the resulting output for subsequent analysis [11]. Simulations are important tools in scientific research as they also enable researchers to predict, test and understand systems before attempting to building them [24]. In general, the output of simulations require interpretation (and visualization) for proper or adequate relation to real world situations.

In different domains of science, physical experiments such as the LHC (CERN, Geneva), Genome related sequencing and planned SKA, are already producing massive volumes of data. Research output from both simulations and physical experiments have increased exponentially in volume (and dimension) thanks to the demand for increasing complex simulations as well as the need to study and analyze things with higher fine-grain resolutions. Graphical visualization of voluminous or large or big datasets for research is becoming increasing challenging even when it is often the only useful means of ensuring better comprehension of otherwise numeric data. In addition, deriving adequate cognitive development from these outputs requires the ability to interact with and explore the data to a much higher level or degree. As shown, in Fig. 1, some presentation formats such as simulations permit higher levels of inherent interactivity.

This paper presents a technique for the visualization of research data with higher interactivity. The rest of this paper is organised as follows, Sect. 2 discusses a mobile scope for Augmented Reality technology in relation to Virtual Reality. Section 3 presents the visualization of research data using mobile Augmented Reality in the form of two use-cases. Section 4 concludes this paper after presenting the future work.

2   Background

In psychology and education, learning theories exists to explain and predict how individuals are expected to learn and/or progress in learning. Learning theories provide perspectives and useful insight into the complex process of acquiring knowledge, covering areas such as content design (curriculum), delivery (teaching) and phased growth. Behaviourism as a Learning Theory focuses on how knowledge may be obtained or behaviour changed through conditioning mainly by external stimuli such as rewards or punishments. Radical behaviourism [33] uses operant conditioning which is more about how the response to stimuli operates on the environment and does not require the preexistence of a natural behaviour as in classical conditioning.

In operant conditioning, the acquisition of new behaviour occurs though conditioning stimuli with repeat operations suitable for reinforcing the behaviour or correction operations that punish in order to reduce wrong behaviour or extinction [37] operations that ignore wrong behaviour until it dies. Behaviourism is a central theory in the development of educational software and/or computer based aids for learning as most educational software packages employ the principles of rewarding and enforcing correct answers (behaviour).

The learning theory of Cognitivism focuses on the study of three different unseen states/items: the mental states, how the mind grows, and the ability of individuals to understand. All three are states/items that cannot be measured directly (normally) and always have to inferred or deduced from the interaction with the environment. Similar to behaviourism, cognitivism also deals with the response to the environment and Piaget, a major proponent of cognitivism identified four distinct stages of cognitive development (sensormotorial, preoperational, concrete operational and formal operational) through which individuals pass as they grow (in age). Although, the rate at which an individual passes through a stage varies from one person to another. An association of the four stages with age is found in [9]. In cognitivism, learning occurs primarily through the process of assimilation and accommodation of new knowledge. The learner is viewed as active and very much involved in acting on his/her environment to understand it, changing personal perceptions in order to maintain equilibrium with current knowledge or chooses to assimilate or accommodate new information [18].

The work discussed in this paper involve the presentation of research data outputs using ICT tools with enhanced interactivity for researchers to actively engage with the data as this contributes to cognitive development. Virtual Reality (VR) and similar emerging technologies have demonstrated superiority over the traditional Human Computer Interface (HCI) of an alphanumeric keyboard and Visual Display Unit (VDU) with a pointing device (mouse) [34]. Broadly speaking, VR as a technology seeks to facilitate 3D interactions with a computer in new ways. In VR, the goal is to completely replace the real (physical) environment around a user with a computer generated or virtual one, where the user is still able to perceive and interact with objects using the human senses of sight, sound and touch as suitable haptic devices allow users to touch surfaces, grasp and move virtual objects as well as obtain feedback/reactions from them [6, 40].

In scientific research, VR systems have reportedly been used in the simulation of complex (multi-user) systems, in fast or slow time and with a high degree of interactivity [11, 38]. The 3D computer-generated environment provided by VR allows users to interact at various levels in a more natural manner using interface devices and peripherals such as 3D eye-wear and trackers [11]. In mainstream computing, aspects of VR related research such as voice and gesture based computing are allowing computers and ICT devices to use audible instructions and complex sequences of motion as inputs. In this section, we discuss a VR related technology known as Augmented Reality and its cost effective deployment on mobile platforms.

Augmented Reality (AR) is defined as the real-time integration of virtual (computer-generated) objects and information into a three dimensional real world environment [5, 28]. Visually, AR may be considered as a form of VR in which the user has a clear (transparent) view of the real world. However, unlike in VR, where the goal is to completely immerse the user in the virtual environment, the goal in AR is to blend the virtual objects into the real world in order to enhance or compliment the real world objects and provide a semi-immersive or a window-in-the-world kind of experience. Just like VR, AR is not limited to the visual domain as augmentation is possible in the audible or haptic domains. For example, audible sound with spatial effects may be used to indicate direction, that is, sound effects growing louder (in intensity and volume) as the hearer approaches may be used to show correct direction [46].

In AR, the combination of real/virtual objects into a seamless view and management of all interactions (between real and virtual objects as well as between end-user and virtual objects) happens in real time.

There are several examples of the use of AR and related technologies for cognitive development. For example, it has been used to study human behaviour [15], reconstruction of heritage [19], teach specific procedures to pilots, doctors and operators [17, 31, 32, 36], simulate experiments in chemistry [16], visits to museums and historic buildings [44] and visualization of complex organs within the human body as well as for medical training [1]. An AR application was used to interactively study web-based 3D model of piston in mechanical engineering [22]. Another example involved the use of head mounted (see-through) AR viewer to augment a normal story book providing a 3D animated view of the characters from the story book [8]. In all these examples, the use of AR and/or related technology stimulated cognitive development (prior knowledge [35] and academic engagement [39]) and eliminated the associated risks involved with studying them in real world situations.

In this paper, we consider only see-through [5] AR, where real world view of the surrounding environment (obtained from a live video feed or camera-sensor) is shown directly on the display medium as this is the predominant form on mobile or portable devices.

2.1 Cost Effective Mobile AR

AR and related technologies has always been considered expensive, due to their use of highly specialized equipment such as display walls, specialized projection devices, head-mounted displays (HMD), back-pack computing platforms and other custom equipment [12, 26, 28]. In this work, the term mobile AR is limited to cover only its use on portable consumer grade ICT devices such as smart-phones/tablets and their specialized peripherals such as head or chest mounting units, glasses and watches. That is, we focus on commodity mobile devices such as smart-phones and tablets and achieve cost effectiveness by eliminating the use of custom (expensive) hardware and equipment [14].

Mobile AR on smart-phones rely on the in-built loudspeaker(s), display-screen and the ability to vibrate for auditory, visual and haptic augmentations respectively, while input (and feedback from user) may be derived from a rich array of sensors such as microphone, multi-touch input (display), camera, location (gps), accelerometer, ambient light sensor [14]. Also, touchscreen enabled smart-phones/tables devices allow input in the form of gestures and movements that enhance the ability to interact. For example, an expanding two-finger motion is commonly used to achieve a close-up or zooming-in effect. Improvements in mobile-device technology in areas such as vision, interfacing [20] and sensor accuracy are also readily translated to improvements in mobile AR.

Developing AR enabled applications on mobile platforms has been simplified by the availability of standard Application Programming Interfaces (API), libraries, frameworks and Software Development Kits (SDK). The latter offers a hardware-abstracted solution in form of a high-level API that can compensating for many types of problems [25]. For example, the free Android SDK provides manufacturer independent tools and interfaces for programming or developing software for all smart-phones running the Android Operating System [13], while also addressing inconsistent hardware behavior even for commons problems such as poor camera resolution due to distance, motion blur and poor lighting/contrast situations. The free android SDK already contains some 3D/image-processing functions, however other more specialized AR libraries are commonly used [21, 45].

Mobile AR have been used for experiments in electronics [29], power [27] and communications engineering [28], while mobiles devices have been employed in the processing and display of data [13].

3   Visualization of Research Data

As already demonstrated by LHC and genome-sequencing, large-scale scientific experiments in diverse fields are capable of generating massive volumes of data, while on the other-hand, the availability and increasing use of Internet of Things (IoT) sensors for data acquisition is also generating high velocity data in a wide variety of formats. Researchers are increasingly tasked with processing, understanding and deriving new meanings from voluminous data and/or high speed data in a variety of formats. Computers and other ICT tools play an ever increasing role in the generation, acquisition and high performance processing of voluminous data. In these cases, computer based visualization plays a fundamental role in making sense from data and using emerging (already available) technologies such as Virtual Reality (VR) and Augmented Reality (AR) can provide and support richer interactions with computers especially suited for a 3D environment and/or experience. A visionary look at computing suggests a future where multiple devices seamlessly collaborate to improve our everyday life. While the growing use of interactive surfaces on devices such as laptops, smart-boards, car entertainment/ navigation systems, fitness monitoring devices and of-course smart-phones/tables, is a step in this direction, it is clear that their integration is hardly seamless as data is still largely bounded to individual applications, devices and services.

As discussed in preceding sections, the interactive visualization of data enhances the ability to stimulate cognitive development and application in research environments have largely focused on room-scale visualization using Computer Assisted Virtual Environments (CAVEs) based on the VR philosophy of a completely virtualized environment. A modern room-scale environment, the Wall-sized Interaction with Large Datasets (WILD) room is presented in [7]. Where a wall-sized display is combined with a multitouch table and various mobile devices specifically to help scientists collaborate on the analysis of large and complex datasets. It was envisioned that the WILD room could be used by a group of microbiologist (co-located in the WILD room) to study how one molecule docks with another and interactively and seamlessly switch between several 3D representations, different molecular models, online databases, websites and research articles along with the ability to collaborate with remote colleagues [7].

Creating, programming and operating a room-scale interactive environment for research comes with challenges in developing software application for multi-surface or distributed interactions and rendering as well as obtaining content from multiple sources. Commodity mobile (smartphone and tablet) devices provide a single display environment with multitouch capabilities that is relatively easy to programme. In this section, we discuss the use of mobile AR for presenting research data and provide as examples two specific use-cases: the interactive and immersive visualization of abstract quantities and geophysical data.

Apart from cost effectiveness discussed in Sect. 2, several recent improvements in AR such as the ability to use normal (arbitrary) objects as augmentation marker, advanced tracking of objects, photo-realistic rendering and automatic re-dimensioning of objects contribute to making mobile AR well suited for the visualization of research data.

3.1 Visualization of Abstract Quantities

Understanding the wireless transmission of signals requires studying the propagation of electromagnetic radiation. Typically, this is carried out using antenna radiation plot(s), which is the representation of the magnitude, phase and polarization of the electromagnetic field around an antenna in polar and rectangular coordinates. The plot(s) are equally applicable during either transmission or reception. Both polar and rectangular plots are not readily associated to real-world situations and it is clear that electromagnetic waves are also not visible even when cognitive development includes hands-on practical laboratory exercises. Figure 2 shows the 3D and 2D view of the radiation pattern from a 9-element yagi antenna as produced by a mobile AR application developed as part of a joint collaboration between the Ulster University (UU) and the International Centre for Theoretical Physics (ICTP). In the 2D view (left side of Fig. 2), the light coloured line is the horizontal plane, while the dark coloured line is for the vertical plane.

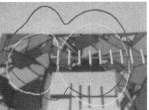

Fig. 2. AR 3D visualization of antenna radiation pattern

The same application was used for the visualization of three different datasets generated from numerical simulations with the 4nec2 [42] software tool; each dataset represented a different type of antenna. The application automatically selected the right datasets based on the recognition of a corresponding AR marker and also included additional contextual controls for interactively changing several parameters including angle of grounding plane, diameter, number of elements and operational frequency, the resulting change in radiation patterns are immediately visible [28].

During viewing, the 3D model dataset ensures researchers can immersively explore the realistic radiation pattern interactively, scaling (zoom) by simply moving the mobile device closer to the marker. The ability to switch between 2D and 3D stimulated better comprehension of antenna radiation patterns and even understanding of the associated plots.

3.2   Visualization of Geophysical Data

During the formation of young researchers in the field of Earth System Physics, they are often faced with studying various land formations and the ability to actually visualize these landforms contributes to their cognitive development.

Figure 3 shows the AR immersive cubicle jointly developed for 3D viewing of geophysical data by Santa's Co (a software development company from Reggio Emilia, Italy), the UU and the ICTP. The semi-immersive AR environment (cubicle) is composed of four markers, while three markers were positioned vertical, the fourth was placed horizontal to provide a 180 + 90° seamless exploratory view of the landforms created from data. That is, 180° radius in the horizontal direction and 90 in the vertical direction.

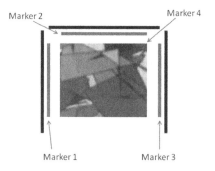

Fig. 3.   AR immersive cubicle.

Figure 4 shows horizontal and vertical view of the landforms using a mobile (tablet) device.

Fig. 4. Mobile AR vertical view of immersive cubicle.

The AR cubicle was used at ICTP for the 3D semi-immersive exploration of research data by researchers and also show-cased at the 2013 Teachers day event, held at UNESCO headquarters, Paris [2, 3].

3.3   User Feedback

Anonymous feedback on the first-time use of the mobile AR visualization tool (first use-case) was obtained from 150 learners from the Obafemi Awolowo University, Nigeria and the Addis Ababa University, Ethiopia. The consenting adult volunteers, who participated without incentives, risks and disadvantages in the international study were informed of the purpose, confidentiality of the study and the intended use of the collected data. Over 90% of the sample population were from various disciplines of natural sciences and engineering. About 74% were undergraduate students and only 19% were female. Although, the mean age was between 21–24 years, about 70% of respondents were also first-time users of VR and AR technologies.

Participants selected from a 5-scale Likert responses to closed questions on if the AR tool helped their studies or if they became confused after using the AR tool (Table 1).

Table 1.   Was the AR tool helpful to your study?

Response	%
No	18.12
Don't think so	7.38
Can't say	20.81
Somehow	24.83
Definitely	28.86

The feedback obtained from show that over 50% of respondents found the visualization provided by the AR tool helped their studies, only 19.33% found the AR tool confusing and in both questions, 20% and 27% of the respondents were not sure. Additional feedback about the mobile AR CAVE like cubicle was obtained during a public event. The invited dignitaries and high school students provided positive comments on the efficacy of the cubicle for tourism and learning (Table 2).

Table 2. Did you find the AR tool confusing?

Response	%
No	35.33
Don't think so	18.67
Can't say	26.67
Somehow	14.00
Definitely	5.33

The results presented in this section are limited to the specific cognitive tasks/scope described in the use-cases and although based on self-assessments by users, they suggest a positive contribution to cognitive development.

3.4 Strengths and Weaknesses

The visualization of research data could potentially improve and change practices when it is used for navigation through a single large object such as a gigapixel image of deep space; comparison of large numbers of related images, for example brain scans; juxtaposition of a variety of heterogeneous forms of data from different sources, that is, tables, formulas, graphs, photographs and video clips; and for remote collaborative exploration [7].

In both use-cases presented in this paper, mobile AR provides increased interactivity that enabled richer contextually viewing of datasets. The visualization experience is semi-immersive on mobile devices and fully immersive when they are combined with suitable head-mounts. This immersive visualization of datasets enhanced contextual understanding and cognitive development.

The use of AR on commodity ICT devices is cost effective as hardware are readily affordable/available to all and developing corresponding software could be cost-free. Software development is simplified as the application interface was deliberately kept simple to avoid overloading the learner with too much concurrent/contextual information which could harm the cognitive development process [1].

Mitigating two well-known limitations of mobile device involved keeping ambient lighting at normal room levels so learners are not faced with poor visibility on mobile device screens due to strong lighting [14] and addressing the dependency on rechargeable batteries for energy to function required the provision of suitable cables for charging mobile devices as well as factoring in a 20 min period for battery charging of user devices prior to activities.

The limited display/screen size allows only a windowed view of dataset(s), with total size (of all datasets) limited by the storage capacity of individual devices. Complex gestures or movements involving two-hands is not yet possible as learners hold the mobile device in one hand and can only perform gestures with the other hand. The current versions of the mobile AR applications have limited support for group-use or visualization.

4   Future Works and Conclusions

The Artificial Intelligence and Applications Research Group at Ulster University is setting up an Experience Lab, which will include the deployment of cost effective Augmented Reality (AR) cubicles (or CAVEs) at Ulster University and the ICTP. Both groups will investigate creating fully-immersive AR environments using suitable head and chest-mounted mobile devices, this will allow researchers enjoy a 360 immersion exploration of datasets and possible allow the use of both hands for gestural interactions.

In the Information Visualization for Big Data (IVIS4BigData) reference model [48], shown in Fig. 5, multiple researchers in different geographically separate locations are expected to concurrently work together, interactively examining/exploring Big-Data or research data in real-time and without restrictions.

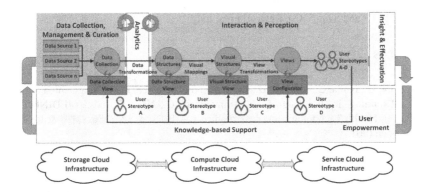

Fig. 5. The IVIS4BigData Reference model. Source: Bornschlegl et al. (2016) [48]

Progressing towards the IVSI4BigData model would require research on various techniques for dynamically transforming and streaming fragments of Big-Data to a variety of visualization tools as described here. In line with the IVIS4BigData reference model, we plan to extend the mobile AR visualization tools for multidisciplinary Computer Supported Group Work (CSCW) based on open standards over various infrastructure including local wireless or mesh networks, the internet and Clouds.

Apart from the above described activities, we foresee the immersive interactive exploration of various datasets from diverse sources within the "Experience Lab". For example, geospatial datasets of existing locations (or cities) could be used to provide interactive remote exploration and tourism related experience. Other datasets derived from Internet of Things (IoT) or other sensors could be used for the interactive exploration and study of otherwise inaccessible locations including underground caves, coral reefs or other seabeds and even in some mining related activities.

4.1 Conclusion

This paper has examined a cost effective use of mobile Augmented Reality (AR) in the visualization of scientific research data. Two use-cases are presented that show the use of a 3D semi-immersive interactive environment provided by mobile AR including a CAVE like AR cubicle, along with some evidence of contribution to cognitive development. While both use-cases showcased applications in the academic domain, the "Experience Lab" at the Ulster University, Belfast is positioned to research and improve on the application of mobile AR technology in line with the IVIS4BigData reference model for diverse kinds of immersive/experiential visualization of academic and non-academic applications in-cluding augmented-videoconferencing, augmented-tourism and augmented-mining.

Acknowledgments. The authors acknowledge the contributions and support of the School of Computing, Ulster University; the Telecommunications and ICT for Development (T/ICT4D) Laboratory, ICTP and Santa's Co, Regio-Emilia, Italy.

References

1. Albrechta, U., Nolla, C., von Jan, U.: Explore and experience: mobile augmented reality for medical training. In: Lehmann, C.U., Ammenwert, C., Nahr, C. (eds.) MEDINFO 2013. Studies in Health Technologis and Informatics, vol. 192, pp. 382–386. IMIE & IOS Press, Copehegen (2013)
2. Annaffismo Innanzitutto [ilsantass]. Santa'S Co. & ICTP at World Teachers Day 2013 - UNESCO - Paris - AR Cave - Part 1, October 2013. http://www.youtube.com/watch?v=Gr4_zuMl_qM. Accessed 15 Nov 2013
3. Annaffismo Innanzitutto [ilsantass]. Santa'S Co. & ICTP at World Teachers Day 2013 - UNESCO - Paris - AR Seeduino Board - Part 2, October 2013. http://www.youtube.com/watch?v=rxFM7ZA8c. Accessed 15 Nov 2013
4. Aung, W., Llic, V., Mertanen, O., Moscinski, J., Uhomoibhi, J. (eds.): Innovations 2012: World Innovations in Engineering Education and Research. iNEER, Potomac (2012)
5. Azuma, R., Baillot, Y., Behringer, R., Feiner, S., Julier, S., MacInTyre, B.: Recent advances in augmented reality. IEEE Comput. Graph. Appl. **21**(6), 34–47 (2001)
6. Basdogan, C., Ho, C.-H., Srinivasan, M.A., Slater, M.: An experimental study on the role of touch in shared virtual environments. ACM Trans. Comput. Hum. Interact. **7**(4), 443–460 (2000)
7. Beaudouin-Lafon, M., Huot, S., Nancel, M., Mackay, W., Pietriga, E., Primet, R., Wagner, J., Chapuis, O., Pillias, C., Eagan, J., Gjerlufsen, T., Klokmose, C.: Multisurface interaction in the wild room. Computer **45**(4), 48–56 (2012)
8. Billinghurst, M., Kato, H., Poupyrev, I.: The magicbook - moving seamlessly between reality and virtuality. IEEE Comput. Graph. Appl. **21**(3), 6–8 (2001)
9. Bybee, R., Sund, R.: Piaget for Educators, 2nd edn. Charles E. Merril Publishing Company, New York (1982)
10. Canessa, E., Zennaro, M.: A mobile science index for development. Int. J. Interact. Mobile Technol. **6**(1), 4–6 (2012)
11. Cecil, J.: The creation of virtual learning environments. In: Aung et al. [4], pp. 263–273

12. Davidsson, M., Johansson, D., Lindwall, K.: Exploring the use of augmented reality to support science education in secondary schools. In: Seventh International Conference on Wireless, Mobile and Ubiquitous Technology in Education, pp. 218–220. IEEE Computer Society (2012)

13. Fiawoo, S., Sowah, R.: Design and development of an android application to process and display summarised corporate data. In: 2012 IEEE 4th International Conference on Adaptive Science Technology (ICAST), pp. 86–91, October 2012

14. FitzGerald, E., Adams, A., Ferguson, R., Gaved, M., Mor, Y., Thomas, R.: Augmented reality and mobile learning: the state of the art. In: Specht, M., Sharples, M., Multisilta, J. (eds.) 11th World Conference on Mobile and Contextual Learning (mLearn 2012), pp. 62–69. CEUR, Helsinki (2012)

15. Fox, J., Arena, B., Bailenson, J.N.: Virtual reality: a survival guide for the social scientist. J. Media Psychol. 21(3), 95–113 (2009)

16. Georgiou, J., Dimitropoulos, K., Manitsaris, A.: A virtual reality laboratory for distance education in chemistry. 1(11), 337–344 (2007)

17. Henderson, S.J., Feiner, S.: Evaluating the benefits of augmented reality for task localization in maintenance of an armored personnel carrier turret. In: Proceedings of IEEE ISMAR-AMH, pp. 135–144. IEEE (2009)

18. Henson, K.T., Eller, B.F.: Educational Psychology for Effective Teaching. Wadsworth, Belmont (1999)

19. Huang, Y., Liu, Y., Wang, Y.: Ar-view: an augmented reality device for digital reconstruction of yuangmingyuan. In: Proceedings of IEEE ISMAR-AMH, pp. 3–7. IEEE (2009)

20. Kilby, J., Gray, K., Elliott, K., Waycott, J., Sanchez, F.M., Dave, B.: Designing a mobile augmented reality tool for the locative visualization of biomedical knowledge. In: Lehmann, C., Ammenwert, C., Nahr, C. (eds.) MEDINFO 2013. Studies in Health Technologis and Informatics, vol. 192, pp. 652–656. IMIE & IOS Press, Copenhagen (2013)

21. Kim, S.L., Suk, H.J., Kang, J.H., Jung, J.M., Laine, T., Westlin, J.: Using unity 3D to facilitate mobile augmented reality game development. In: 2014 IEEE World Forum on Internet of Things (WF-IoT), pp. 21–26, March 2014

22. Liarokapis, F., Mourkoussis, N., White, M., Darcy, J., Sifniotis, M., Petridis, P., Basu, A., Lister, P.F.: Web3D and augmented reality to support engineering education. World Trans. Eng. Technol. Educ. 3(1), 11–14 (2004)

23. McMillan, S.J., Hoy, M.G., Kim, J., McMahan, C.: A multifaceted tool for a complex phenomenon: coding web-based interactivity as technologies for interaction evolve. J. Comput. Mediated Commun. 13(4), 794–826 (2008)

24. Moeller, P.F.D., Drews, A., Selke, G.: Micro-magnetic simulations in research-based engineering education. In: Aung et al. [4], pp. 1–15

25. Mutholib, A., Gunawan, T., Kartiwi, M.: Design and implementation of automatic number plate recognition on android platform. In: 2012 International Conference on Computer and Communication Engineering (ICCCE), pp. 540–543, July 2012

26. Onime, C., Abiona, O.: 3D mobile augmented reality interface for laboratory experiments. Int. J. Commun. Netw. Syst. Sci. 09(04), 67–76 (2016)

27. Onime, C., Uhomoibhi, J., Pietrosemoli, E.: An augmented virtuality based solar energy power calculator in electrical engineering. Int. J. Eng. Pedagogy 5(1), 4–7 (2015)

28. Onime, C., Uhomoibhi, J., Radicella, S.: Mare: mobile augmented reality based experiments in science, technology and engineering. In: Restivo, M.T.R., Cardoso, A., Lopez, A.M. (eds.) Online Experimentation: Emerging Technologies and IoT. IFSA Publishing, Barcelona (2015)

29. Onime, C., Uhomoibhi, J., Zennaro, M.: A low cost implementation of an existing hands-on laboratory experiment in electronic engineering. Int. J. Eng. Pedagogy **4**(4), 1–3 (2014)
30. Onime, C.E., Uhomoibhi, J.O.: Using interactive video for online blended learning in engineering education. In: 2013 2nd International Conference on Experiment@ (exp.at 2013), pp. 128–132, September 2013
31. O'Toole, R., Playter, R., Krummel, T., Blank, W., Cornelius, N., Roberts, W., Bell, W., Raibert, M.: Assessing skill and learning in surgeons and medical students using a force feedback surgical simulator. In: Wells, W.M., Colchester, A., Delp, S. (eds.) MICCAI 1998. LNCS, vol. 1496, pp. 899–909. Springer, Heidelberg (1998). doi:10.1007/BFb0056278
32. Pausch, R., Conway, M., Zennaro, M.: A literature survey for virtual environments: military flight simulator visual systems and simulator sickness. Presence: Teleoper. Virtual Environ. **1**(3), 344–363 (1962)
33. Phillips, D.C., Soltis, J.F.: Perspectives in Learning. Teacher's College Press, New York (1998)
34. Rodigues, F., Sato, F., Botega, L., Oliveira, A.: Integration framework of augmented reality and tangible interfaces for enhancing the user interaction. In: 2012 14th Symposium on Virtual and Augmented Reality (SVR), pp. 100–107, May 2012
35. Schmalstieg, D., Wagner, D.: Experiences with handwith augmented reality. In: 6th IEEE and ACM International Symposium on Mixed and Augmented Reality, Japan, pp. 1–13 (2007)
36. Schwald, B., de Laval, B.: An augmented reality system for training and assistance to maintenance in the industrial context. In: Proceedings of International Conference on Computer Graphics, Visualization and Computer Vision, pp. 425–432. IEEE Computer Society (2003)
37. Skinner, B.: The Shaping of a Behaviorist: Part Two of An Autobiography. A Borzoi book. Knopf Doubleday Publishing Group, New York (1979)
38. Sobota, B., Korecko, S., Hrozek, F.: Mobile mixed reality. In: 2013 IEEE 11th International Conference on Emerging eLearning Technologies and Applications (ICETA), pp. 355–358, October 2013
39. Squire, K., Klopfer, E.: Augmented reality simulations on handheld computers. J. Learn. Sci. **16**(3), 371–413 (2007)
40. Tan, H., Pentland, A.: Tactual displays for wearable computing. Pers. Technol. **1**, 225–230 (1997)
41. van Erp, J., Lotte, F., Tangermann, M.: Brain-computer interfaces: beyond medical applications. Computer **45**(4), 26–34 (2012)
42. Voors, A.: 4nec2 antenna modeler and optimizer, October 2012. http://www.qsl.net/4nec2/. Accessed 8 Jan 2014
43. Wells, J., Berry, R.M., Spence, A.: Using video tutorials as a carrot-and-stick approach to learning. IEEE Trans. Educ. **55**(2), 453–458 (2012)
44. White, M., Mourkoussis, N., Darcy, J., Petridis, P., Liarokapis, F., Lister, P., Walczak, K., Wojciechowski, K., Cellary, W., Chmielewski, J., Stawniak, M., Wiza, W., Patel, M., Stevenson, J., Manley, J., Giorgini, F., Sayd, P., Gaspard, F.: Arcoan architecture for digitization, management and presentation of virtual exhibitions. In: Computer Graphics International, pp. 622–625. IEEE, Crete (2004)
45. Xiao, C., Lifeng, Z.: Implementation of mobile augmented reality based on Vuforia and Rawajali. In: 2014 5th IEEE International Conference on Software Engineering and Service Science (ICSESS), pp. 912–915, June 2014
46. Zahorik, P.: Assessing auditory distance perception using virtual acoustics. J. Acoust. Soc. Am. **111**, 1832–1846 (2002)

47. Zennaro, M., Fonda, C.: Radio Laboratory Handbook. ICTP - The Abdus Salam International Centre for Theoretical Physics (2004). http://wireless.ictp.it/handbook/Handbook.pdf
48. Bornschlegl, M.X., Berwind, K., Kaufmann, M., Engel, F.C., Walsh, P., Hemmje, M.L., Riestra, R., Werkmann, B.: IVIS4BigData: a reference model for advanced visual interfaces supporting big data analysis in virtual research environments. In: Bornschlegl, M.X., et al. (eds.) AVI-BDA 2016. LNCS, vol. 10084, pp. 1–18. Springer, Heidelberg (2016)

Visualizing Next-Generation Sequencing Cancer Data Sets with Cloud Computing

Paul Walsh[1(✉)], Brendan Lawlor[1], Brian Kelly[1], Timmy Manning[1], Timm Heuss[2], and Markus Leopold[2]

[1] NSilico Lifescience, Rubicon Centre, CIT Campus, Bishopstown, Cork, Ireland
{paul.walsh,brendan.lawlor,brian.kelly,
timmy.manning}@nsilico.com
[2] University of Applied Sciences Darmstadt, Darmstadt, Germany
{timm.heuss,markus.leopold}@h-da.de

Abstract. With the advent of next-generation sequencing technology, clinical data sets now contain enormous amounts of valuable genomic information related to a wide range of diseases such as cancer. This data needs to be analysed, managed, stored, visualized and integrated in order to be clinically useful. However, many clinicians and researchers, who need to interpret these data sets, are non-specialists in the information technology domain and so need systems that are effective and easy to use. Herein, we present an overview of a novel cloud computing based next-generation sequencing research management software system which has simplicity, scalability, speed and reproducibility at its core. A prototype that enables rapid visualization of big data cancer sets is described. We present preliminary results from a bioinformatics pipeline for the *Sage Care* project, a European Union funded cancer research project, for comprehensive genome mapping analysis and visualization and outlined benefits of integrating this into a graphical user interface platform such as *Simplicity*.

1 Introduction

Many individual laboratories are now able to access technology for generating complex next-generation sequencing (NGS) data sets at affordable prices [1]. These datasets can be enormous given that sequencing a single human genome can require approximately 300 GB of storage [2]. Even basic analysis using simple pattern matching algorithms on just 1 GB of such data typically requires many hours of compute time, see [3] for technical details. For health applications the DNA sequencing of clinical samples can routinely consume 1 TB of storage space, hence one million genomes will require 1 million terabytes, equivalent to 1000 PB or 1 EB [4]. It is also well documented that such growth in data sets will be accelerated by further efficiencies in sequencing technologies that can scan entire genomes directly for around US$100 [1]. Dealing with this exponential growth presents a major limiting factor to many research laboratories. While many large institutes can afford dedicated high performance computing systems, smaller research teams cannot access the same level of resources [5].

© Springer International Publishing AG 2016
M.X. Bornschlegl et al. (Eds.): AVI-BDA 2016, LNCS 10084, pp. 50–62, 2016.
DOI: 10.1007/978-3-319-50070-6_4

At the same time, melanoma, which is a malignant tumour of melanocytes, presents with about 160,000 new cases diagnosed annually among Europeans [6]. This is a serious health issue and this research aims to impact the treatment of this disease by providing a visualisation platform that allows researchers to rapidly query and review integrated genomic datasets. This would provide a basis for personalised treatments by allowing health professionals to interrogate holistic information sources. This aligns with an actual clinical need to extract as much meaning as possible from biomedical data, by linking and analysing genomic, research and electronic health record (EHR) data for cancer management.

Although tools already exist that can provide such visualization, major challenges in the widespread adoption of such visualisation techniques exist due to, inter alia, their complex computational characteristics, the need for software tools that are usable for both researchers and clinicians and the need for software solutions that are secure and auditable, providing full traceability and provenance of data. Therefore, the principal objective of the discussion presented in this paper is to design easy-to-use in silico techniques that can support the rapid analysis and visualisation of bioinformatics data-sets and to embed these techniques in an efficient, usable, auditable and secure end-to-end diagnostic process.

1.1   Cloud Based Solutions

Cloud computing promises ubiquitous high-throughput analytics that will allow users to interrogate the data more rapidly and to accurately and efficiently infer relationships between large data sets. We define cloud computing as 'computing capability that abstracts the underlying hardware architectures, enabling convenient, on-demand network access to a shared pool of computing resources that can be readily provisioned and released' (based on NIST Technical Report [7]). Cloud computing allows the extensive storage capacity and RAM needed for genetic research to be accessible in a scalable fashion without the need for expensive fixed capital costs. It makes more sense to acquire such resources on a pay-per-use basis via cloud computing models such as infrastructure as a service (IaaS), platform as a service (PaaS) or software as a service (SaaS). Such models provide a more democratic approach where shared public infrastructure is made available to many more users via shared costs.

1.2   Leveraging Cloud Technology

Migration to high performance computing, while clearly advantageous, raises a new set of challenges that must be met in order to leverage the benefits of cloud technology [8]. In order to avail of this infrastructure, bioinformatics applications must be designed to be parallelised in nature and this requires specialist knowledge of data intensive computing frameworks. One such typical framework is Hadoop which reduces 100's of hours of wait time into only a few hours [9]. But a documented drawback of such HPC systems is that they require the expertise of computing specialists to implement and maintain. Moreover, Hadoop assumes that the problem or question can principally be solved in a Map-Reduce approach. Cloud-based bioinformatics software tools are emerging rapidly but do not yet address sufficiently the need to integrate the various disparate cloud-based software systems. A typical bioinformatics task requires biologists to manually and repeatedly co-ordinate multiple software systems to produce a result [10]. An example of such a task would be to use different bioinformatics tools in succession to produce the required data. As each tool returns data, the biologist must manually clean and format the data to ensure compatibility with the next tool. If such tools are based on the cloud then it requires repeated transfer of large data sets both to and from the cloud. These activities are time consuming, error prone and hard to retrace. One way to address these issues is to develop bioinformatics pipeline tools that automate the integration of various steps [10]. We believe that such tools can have even greater impact if they provide an intuitive interface to specify parallel streams of execution. Indeed, if our objective of democratizing the access to such cloud computing tools is to be realized then it is of vital importance that user intuitive interfaces and features are provided to realize the widespread use of these applications.

1.3 Managing Big Data Using Pipelines

The last decade has seen a significant uptake of next generation sequencing, which is a technology capable of digitizing vast amounts of DNA, RNA, and other high throughput technologies that has led to an enormous increase in the amount of biological data held in publically available databases [11]. Processing of this genomic 'big data' using bioinformatics is now a core skill for life science researchers who spend a significant part of their time at the bench and at a computer [12]. There are many web and desktop tools available for a researcher to complete bioinformatics tasks, that may require users to manually and repeatedly co-ordinate multiple tools to produce the required data [13]. As a result many pipeline tools have been developed to automate these tasks using web services. However, most of these tools are tailored for specialist bioinformaticians or are unstable and may require too much time to learn; as a consequence, many life science researchers fail to engage with these pipeline tools. Indeed, it is shown that usability problems can pose significant obstacles to a satisfactory user experience and force researchers to spend unnecessary time and effort to complete their tasks [14].

2 Methods

We present a prototype solution, which we call Simplicity[1], which puts the usability of cloud-based high performance computation first and foremost, while providing full traceability and provenance while generating detailed reports via the big data capability of the cloud. Our goal for such a system is the provision of advanced cloud-based informatics for clinical researchers in the medical diagnostics space that provides a pay-per-use service that eliminates high capital cost and offers easy access to high performance algorithms by shielding users from their underlying complexities. A fully editable, detailed report allows the user to review pipeline results for all tools by providing tables

---

[1] *Simplicity* is a trademark *NSilico* Lifescience Ltd.

and charts where possible. In our current work we are in the process of extending this approach to the rapid analysis and visualisation of cancer datasets.

2.1 Architecture

The architecture of a cloud computing based system that supports these goals is based on a service oriented architecture (SOA) [15] that leverages the capabilities of either public or private cloud platforms or a hybrid configuration of both. A public cloud is one based on the standard cloud computing model, in which a service provider makes resources, such as computing, applications and storage available to the general public over the Internet and typically use a pay-per-usage model. A private cloud is infrastructure operated solely for a single organization, whether managed internally or by a third-party and hosted internally or externally. As the core backend is executed in a Docker container (https://www.docker.com), the system can be deployed and scaled on arbitrary cloud infrastructure such as Windows Azure (http://www.windowsazure.com/en-us/) and Amazon EC2 (http://aws.amazon.com/ec2/) (see Fig. 1).

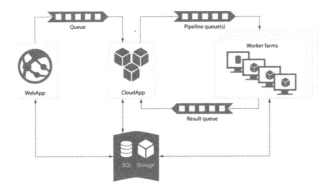

Fig. 1. Simplicity cloud architecture

The pay-per-use model of the public cloud model offering has removed the up-front capital costs for users, thus enabling organisations to "start small" and increase hardware resources only when there is an increase in their needs. The option allows users to pay for use of infrastructure as it is required and, perhaps more importantly, de-allocate such resources and their associated costs when they are no longer needed [16].

Simplicity addresses access to economically accessible high performance computation resources by the methodical development of highly usable cloud-based software tools. Users simply select analytical tools from a list and Simplicity will manage the interoperability of the tools automatically. Arranging tools in parallel implicitly causes them to run multiple instances of processes in parallel within the cloud infrastructure. Moreover, users can implicitly invoke massive parallelism by enabling cloud-supported implementations of tools such as Bowtie on Windows Azure, Amazon EC2 and private cloud instances [17]. The Simplicity system is also highly asynchronous as users can launch complex jobs and be notified by email when results are ready. Such ease of use

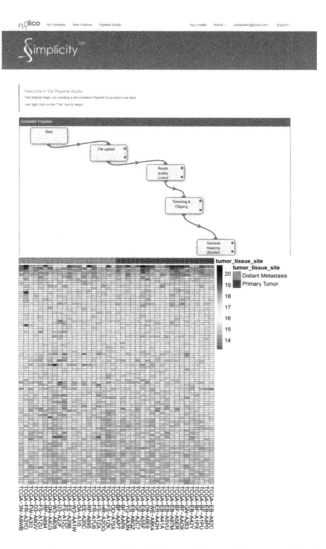

Fig. 2. A mockup of the proposed *Simplicity* platform pipeline showing how complex bioinformatics pipelines can be easily run and visualised with simple "mouse-click" selection, using open source packages such as DeSEQ2 and edgeR, without the need for programming expertise.

can potentially bring powerful bioinformatics tools into the hands of researchers who do not have the financial resources of larger research institutions, by either leveraging the pay-per-use model of public cloud or by deploying the system to a private cloud implementation of low cost commodity servers.

2.2 User Centered Design

The prototype system was designed for the cloud using user centered design approach along with an agile programming methodology [18]. Requirements were gathered from over 100 biologists and bioinformaticians from several university research labs, hospitals and diagnostics companies about what features they would like to see in a bioinformatics pipeline tool.

In user-centred design it is important to understand who the target users are, the kind of tasks these users wish to perform with the software and also what environment will the software be used in. To understand what tasks users perform in bioinformatics and also what tools they use to perform these tasks, interviews, focus groups, feature analysis and cognitive walkthroughs were undertaken. An online survey was also conducted to get feedback from the bioinformatics community.

Information on users was collected using various qualitative and quantitative research methods. Qualitative research methods including focus groups and interviews were carried out with target users. These methods while being highly subjective are designed to look beyond the percentages to gain an understanding of the customer's feelings, impressions and viewpoints. Quantitative research methods were also carried out using competitive analysis and online surveys.

2.3 Users and Environment

Researchers in the life sciences in both academia and industry were asked questions about their studies, general computer experience, bioinformatics training and attitude towards bioinformatics. The researchers taking part in the requirements gathering were typically: micro or molecular biologists, mid-twenties to early thirties in age, honours degree, masters or PhD, have a working knowledge of Microsoft Windows and Microsoft Office and would regard themselves as having little to adequate experience in bioinformatics. Most of those who responded to the survey work in a research capacity (see Fig. 3). The researchers had no formal training in using bioinformatics tools; such skills were picked up from other biologists or learned by doing online tutorials about tool use. Some comments people had were "easy to get frustrated, you need patience", "repetitive work", "don't mind using programs once they save time" and "would rather do wet lab work". Nearly all the researchers would like to learn more about bioinformatics as it is becoming a central tool in biology.

Of those surveyed, the majority had an active interest in the field of transcriptomics (see Fig. 4), which is the study of the expression of messenger RNA molecules expressed from the genes of an organism and their functions. Researchers typically investigate transcriptome changes across a variety of biological conditions, for example the difference between tumour gene expression levels from patients. These areas of activity are closely followed by bioinformatic analysis related to the analysis of genomes. Simplicity has been engineered to provide support for the development of such activity.

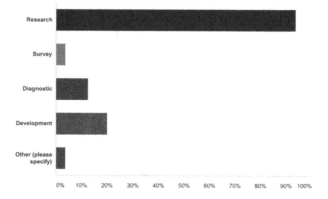

Fig. 3. The primary activity of those who responded to the survey.

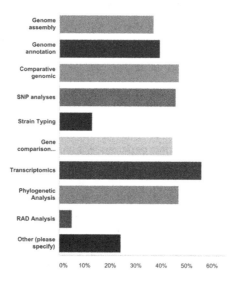

Fig. 4. Main bioinformatics activity of those surveyed.

Reproducibility was also a major issue which came to the fore through literature review and survey. Of those surveys over 83% strongly agreed that reproducibility is a core concern in bioinformatics. Reproducibility is one of the main principles of the scientific method and is defined as the ability of an entire study to be replicated, either by the researcher or by someone else working independently, so as to corroborate the original results. Achieving reproducibility in life science is particularly challenging as even the most basic entities are composed of highly dynamic and interactive complex systems. Issues of reproducibility in life science are now being recognised more widely in both the scientific community and popular press. Recently, biotech company Amgen attempted to replicate the findings of 53 landmark articles published by reputable labs in top journals, but only 6 of the 53 studies were reproduced.

Visualisation is also of major importance and end-users were surveyed about what tools they use for visualisation (see Fig. 5). One of the most popular tools in use amongst respondents is the genome browser known as the Integrative Genomics Viewer (IGV), which is a high-performance visualization tool for interactive exploration of large, integrated genomic datasets. It supports a wide variety of data types, including array-based and next-generation sequence data, and genomic annotations [19]. Another popular tool is Cytoscape, which is an open source software platform for visualizing complex networks and integrating these with any type of attribute data [20]. This has become popular in bioinformatics for visualising gene and protein interactions. Many users expressed a preference for a variety of tools, which upon further probing included spreadsheet and chart based tools which were used to create charts and plots. The simplicity platform has been engineered with such tools in mind as it provides a framework for integrating multiple data sources so they can be visualised through the user's preferred visualisation format.

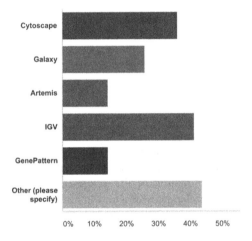

Fig. 5. Main choice of visualisation tool among those surveyed.

These requirements were used to synthesise design specification which resulted in a cloud-based research tool Simplicity. An evaluation of this tool against a real genomics case study on infection has already been carried out. This study indicated that the majority of the findings of a month long manual project by a researcher can be replicated in a matter of hours using this software tool at a relatively low cost [21]. We are now extending this approach to the analysis of cancer datasets and preliminary results from the pipeline are producing reproducible results. This pipeline will ultimately be available to researchers through the drag-and-drop interface of Simplicity as shown on a proof of concept mock-up in Fig. 2. This drag-and-drop interface provides easy-to-use pipeline configuration whereby users with little or no bioinformatics programming can assemble complex pipelines.

Moreover each component of the pipeline can be configured through a simple graphical user interface. For example Fig. 6 shows how a next-generation sequence trimming tool can be easily configured through radio buttons and drop-down text box controls. Trimming tools are commonly used in many pipelines to remove sequencing artefacts from raw reads from sequencing machine such as Illumina HiSeq (http://www.illumina.com/systems/hiseq_2500_1500.html).

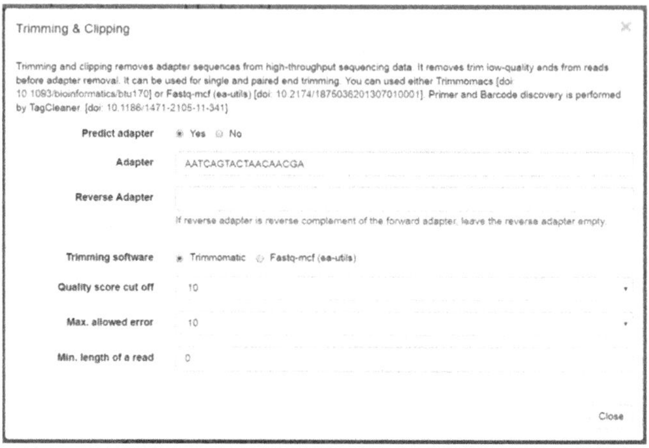

Trimming & Clipping   ✕

Trimming and clipping removes adapter sequences from high-throughput sequencing data. It removes trim low-quality ends from reads before adapter removal. It can be used for single and paired end trimming. You can used either Trimmomacs [doi: 10.1093/bioinformatics/btu170] or Fastq-mcf (ea-utils) [doi: 10.2174/1876036201307010001]. Primer and Barcode discovery is performed by TagCleaner [doi: 10.1186/1471-2105-11-341]

Predict adapter   ◉ Yes ○ No

Adapter   AATCAGTACTAACAACGA

Reverse Adapter

                   If reverse adapter is reverse complement of the forward adapter, leave the reverse adapter empty.

Trimming software ◉ Trimmomatic ○ Fastq-mcf (ea-utils)

Quality score cut off   10

Max. allowed error   10

Min. length of a read   0

                                                                                       Close

Fig. 6. An example of an easily configurable component of a multistage pipeline.

The Simplicity framework also supports the IVIS4BigData Reference Model (see Fig. 7). Handling the large volumes of data typical of bioinformatics requires a structured approach to dealing with access, visualization, perception, and interaction. Current bioinformatics platforms lack uniform and user-centered access to efficient configuration, administration, and exploitation of life science research resources during the execution of cooperative research processes where intermediate results have to be shared between interdisciplinary teams and their organizations. Furthermore, they lack a

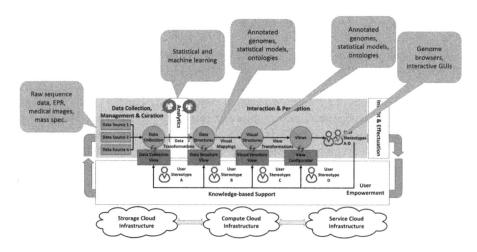

Fig. 7. IVIS4BigData Reference Model

standard service infrastructure supporting the entire life cycle of bioinformatics research and fail to intelligently support integration of diverse research resources. These deficiencies can be alleviated by taking a structured approach – as is done in Simplicity - by mapping the phases of bioinformatics analysis to the IVIS4BigData Reference Model.

2.4 Objectives

The adoption of bioinformatics into mainstream life sciences has seen an increase in the number of tools being developed and maintained by universities, institutes and commercial companies, but the acceptance and use of these tools by biologists lags significantly behind the tool proliferation [22]. The majority of bioinformatics tools are open source (http://www.opensource.org) projects. The term 'open source' has become somewhat of a buzzword in bioinformatics circles. Indeed, freely available software has been a cornerstone of collaborative science for a long time [23], yet despite its success, open source faces a number of fundamental challenges, one of which is the lack of usability for non-technical users compared to commercial software.

To address the usability deficit outlined above, we employed an iterative development methodology for Simplicity where throughout the application development life cycle, from gathering requirements from users to the final deployment of the application [24]. The key concept is that feedback from users on iterative prototypes drives improvements in usability. The goal of this approach is to make cloud-based bioinformatics tools much more usable to life science researchers.

2.5 Benefits

The benefit of using Simplicity is that the expertise and knowledge used to create visualisation pipelines are made available to researchers with little bioinformatics knowledge, while providing the scalability, security and traceability needed for a clinical setting. To this end we are currently extending simplicity with a generic pipeline system for differential expression analysis based on tried and trusted open source packages such as DESeq2 [25] along with supporting software services that aid reproducibility. These well-established packages are generally run via command line statements or by using software development environments such as R studio.

The output shown in Fig. 2 will be easily generated by a GUI based file upload and a minimal number of mouse clicks, thereby allowing end-users who are focused on biology to rapidly view complex gene expression profiles of cancer datasets. In the life sciences, gene expression profiling is the evaluation of the activity of tens of thousands of genes, to create an integrated analysis of biological function via a heat map visualisation. The heat map will be generated by a cloud service that wraps the DeSEQ2 differential expression analysis R package. Consequently, users do not need to spend time learning how to use Unix and how to use the many tools but instead can spend their time analyzing the results. The heatmap in Fig. 2 is currently generated by a chain of tools for data quality assurance, read mapping, count analysis, principle component analysis, differential expression analysis and ultimately summary visualisations.

A prototype pipeline has already been implemented which takes as input two comma separated value files and produces summary analysis and visualisations for a cancer research project that is focused on the rapid analysis of melanoma data sets, known as Sage Care. The heat map shown in Fig. 2 was generated by this pipeline and this pipeline is currently being integrated into the Simplicity platform where it will be readily accessible to biological researchers. This will allow cancer researchers who are not IT savvy to easily access complex analysis and rich visualisations.

Simplicity has the benefit of having resources that many researchers cannot currently access such as the large amounts of computing power and RAM required for assembling high coverage libraries and also annotating against the large genomic databases. This is due to the high capital investment needed for suitable IT infrastructure that can handle bioinformatics big data. Rather users can easily take advantage of a relatively low-cost pay-per-use model.

Moreover Simplicity can save time and money by running pipelines simultaneously and allowing users more time to carry out the other activities of their job. This ease of access to a large number of powerful computational steps goes some way we hope to the democratization of life science in silico research via cloud technology.

3   Summary

Quantitative results have previously shown that creating a pipeline in Simplicity in the cloud is quick and easy, thus allowing researchers to quickly and easily access extensive cloud computing resources that may otherwise be beyond their reach [21]. Usability studies have shown that once users have created one pipeline, subsequent pipelines are created very quickly. Moreover, it is trivial for users to invoke parallelism as Simplicity pipelines are developed by NSilico with parallelism in mind. The automated cloud-based pipelines take only a matter minutes to set up and just a few hours to complete execution. No user interaction is required, freeing the user to perform other work. Users are notified when pipelines have completed, at which point they can begin to review and analyse the information in the editable generated report. Users are quickly able to get a high level overview of data by viewing the report and results for each bioinformatics step. The user can if they wish drill down into results via the Simplicity website.

Given that the data output from lab-based sequencing machines has grown several orders of magnitude over the recent years [26], we hope that cloud-based tools such as *Simplicity* can enable wider access to the scalable resources that the cloud has to offer. Other groups share this vision [27] as it is understood that life scientists are burdened with collection, transferring, managing, analysing, visualising, reproducing [28], reporting and archiving enormous sets of complex heterogeneous data, including scientific literature [29].

Our results indicate that life science researchers can readily access powerful bioinformatics pipeline software using intuitive and easy to use interfaces that do not require users to perform complex data queries or transformations. Moreover the system supports reproducibility as it is trivial to re-run complex pipelines. Full traceability and data provenance is also supported as each step of the process is logged in detail. We now plan to extend this approach to the management of life science big data sets for cancer by integrating the analysis pipeline into Simplicity as envisaged in Fig. 2.

Acknowledgements. Paul Walsh, Brian Kelly, Timm Heuss and Brendan Lawlor are investigators on *Sage Care*, a H2020 MCSA funded project, grant number 644186.

References

1. Schadt, E.E., Linderman, M.D., Sorenson, J., Lee, L., Nolan, G.P.: Computational solutions to large-scale data management and analysis. Nat. Rev. Genet. **11**(9), 647–657 (2010). doi: 10.1038/nrg2857
2. Tsai, E.A., et al.: Bioinformatics workflow for clinical whole genome sequencing at partners healthcare personalized medicine. J. Personal. Med. **6**(1), 12 (2016)
3. Liu, C.M., Wong, T., Wu, E., Luo, R., Yiu, S.M., Li, Y., Wang, B., Yu, C., Chu, X., Zhao, K., Li, R., Lam, T.W.: SOAP3: ultra-fast GPU-based parallel alignment tool for short reads. Bioinformatics **28**(6), 878–879 (2011)
4. Grossman, R.: Managing and Analysing 1,000,000 Genomes, September 2012. http://rgrossman.com/2012/09/18/million-genomes-challeng
5. Foster, I.: Accelerating and democratizing science through cloud-based services. IEEE Internet Comput. **15**(3), 70–73 (2011). ISSN: 1089-7801
6. Whiteman, D.C., Green, A.C., Olsen, C.M.: The growing burden of invasive melanoma: projections of incidence rates and numbers of new cases in six susceptible populations through 2031. J. Investig. Dermatol. (2016). doi:10.1016/j.jid.2016.01.035
7. Mell, P., Grance, T.: The NIST definition of cloud computing, National Institute of Standards and Technology (2011). http://csrc.nist.gov/publications/nistpubs/800-145/SP800-145.pdf
8. Hyek, P.: Cloud computing issues and impacts, Global Technology Industry Discussion Series, E&Y (2011). http://www.ey.com/Publication/vwLUAssets/Cloud_computing_issu es,_impacts_and_insights/$File/Cloud%20computing%20issues%20and%20impacts_14Apr 11.pdf
9. Shvachko, K.: The Hadoop distributed file system. In: 2010 IEEE 26th Symposium, Mass Storage Systems and Technologies (MSST). IEEE (2010)
10. Hull, D., Wolstencroft, K., Stevens, R., Goble, C., Pocock, M.R., Li, P., Oinn, T.: Taverna: a tool for building and running pipelines of services. Nucl. Acids Res. **34**(Web Server issue), 729–732 (2006)
11. Brooksbank, C., Cameron, G., Thornton, J.: The European Bioinformatics Institute's data resources. Nucl. Acids Res. Advance Access (2009). doi:10.1093/nar/gkp986
12. Luscombe, N.M., Greenbaum, D., Gerstein, M.: What is bioinformatics? A proposed definition and overview of the field. Methods Inf. Med. **40**(4), 346–358 (2001)
13. Brazas, M.D., Yamada, J.T., Ouellette, B.F.: Evolution in bioinformatic resources: 2009 update on the bioinformatics links directory. Nucl. Acids Res. **37**, 3–5 (2009)
14. Dudley, J.T., Butte, A.J.: A quick guide for developing effective bioinformatics programming skills. PLoS Comput. Biol. **5**(12), e1000589 (2009)
15. Papazoglou, M.P.: Service-oriented computing: state of the art and research challenges. Computer **40**(11), 38–45 (2007). IEEE Computer Society. ISSN: 0018-9162
16. Armbrust, M., Fox, A., Griffith, R., Joseph, A.D., Katz, R., Konwinski, A., Lee, G., Patterson, D., Rabkin, A., Stoica, I., Zaharia, M.: A view of cloud computing. Commun. ACM **53**(4), 50–58 (2010). doi:10.1145/1721654.1721672

17. Lu, W., Jackson, J., Barga, R.: AzureBlast: a case study of developing science applications on the cloud. In: Proceedings of the 19th ACM International Symposium on High Performance Distributed Computing (HPDC 2010), pp. 413–420. ACM, New York (2010). doi: 10.1145/1851476.1851537
18. Cockburn, A.: Agile Software Development. Addison-Wesley Longman Publishing Co., Inc., Boston (2002)
19. Robinson, J.T., Thorvaldsdóttir, H., Winckler, W., Guttman, M., Lander, E.S., Getz, G., Mesirov, J.P.: Integrative genomics viewer. Nat. Biotechnol. **29**, 24–26 (2011)
20. Shannon, P., Markiel, A., Ozier, O., Baliga, N.S., Wang, J.T., Ramage, D., Amin, N., Schwikowski, B., Ideker, T.: Cytoscape: a software environment for integrated models of biomolecular interaction networks. Genome Res. **13**(11), 2498–2504 (2003)
21. Walsh, P., Carroll, J., Sleator, R.D.: Accelerating in silico research with workflows: a lesson in simplicity. Comput. Biol. Med. **43**(12), 2028–2035 (2013)
22. Shachak, A., Shuval, K., Fine, S.: Barriers and enablers to the acceptance of bioinformatics tools: a qualitative study. J. Med. Libr. Assoc. **95**(4), 454–458 (2007)
23. Stajich, J., Lapp, H.: Open source tools and toolkits for bioinformatics: significance, and where are we? Brief. Bioinform. **7**(3), 287–296 (2006)
24. Greene, S., Jones, L., Matchen, P., Thomas, J.: Iterative development in the field. IBM Syst. J. **42**(4), 594–612 (2003)
25. Love, M., Anders, S., Huber, W.: Differential analysis of count data–the DESeq2 package. Genome Biol. **15**, 550 (2014)
26. Kahn, S.D.: On the future of genomic data. Science **331**(6018), 728–729 (2011)
27. Foster, I.: Globus online: accelerating and democratizing science through cloud-based services. In: Internet Computing. IEEE, May–June 2011
28. Nekrutenko, A., Taylor, J.: Next-generation sequencing data interpretation: enhancing reproducibility and accessibility. Nat. Rev. Genet. **13**(9), 667–672 (2012)
29. Evans, J.A., Foster, J.G.: Metaknowledge. Science **331**(6018), 721–725 (2011)

SenseCare: Towards an Experimental Platform for Home-Based, Visualisation of Emotional States of People with Dementia

Felix Engel[1], Raymond Bond[2(✉)], Alfie Keary[3], Maurice Mulvenna[2],
Paul Walsh[3,4], Huiru Zheng[2], Haiying Wang[2], Ulrich Kowohl[5],
and Matthias Hemmje[1]

[1] Research Institute for Telecommunication and Cooperation,
Dortmund, Germany
{fengel,mhemmje}@ftk.de
[2] Ulster University, Newtownabbey, Northern Ireland
{rb.bond,md.mulvenna,h.zheng,hy.wang}@ulster.ac.uk
[3] CIT Informatics, Cork Institute of Technology, Cork, Ireland
alphonsus.keary@mycit.ie
[4] NSilico Life Science, Dublin 4, Ireland
paul.walsh@nsilico.com
[5] Faculty of Mathematics and Computer Science,
University of Hagen, Hagen, Germany

Abstract. Analytics and visualisation of Big Data appearance is still a challenging task. In this paper, the management and visualisation of big data streams will be discussed at hand of data that comes into existence during the care of people with dementia in their own homes. Therein, basic requirements are explored towards the development of a data management, analytics and visualisation platform stemming from application scenarios in which various data streams are created, processed, analysed, visualised and stored for *ad hoc* or later reuse. The platform will be realised on open ICT standards, implemented within the EC co funded SenseCare project.

Keywords: Information visualisation · Interactive visualisation · Emotional signals · SenseCare platform · Affective computing

1 Introduction

Sensor Enabled Affective Computing for Enhancing Medical Care (SenseCare) is an European Union (EU) co funded project, which aims to provide a new affective computing platform based on an information and knowledge ecosystem providing software services applied to the care of people with dementia. In this connected health domain enormous potential and opportunities exist in relation to providing insight, intelligence and assistance to medical professionals, care givers and people with dementia on emotional states and overall holistic wellbeing. The SenseCare platform will integrate data streams from multiple sensors (for example: video frames for facial recognition of emotional states, sensory wearables for physiological emotion analytics,

© Springer International Publishing AG 2016
M.X. Bornschlegl et al. (Eds.): AVI-BDA 2016, LNCS 10084, pp. 63–74, 2016.
DOI: 10.1007/978-3-319-50070-6_5

and other) and will fuse these streams to provide a global assessment that includes objective levels of wellbeing and emotional state.

The most frequently identified unmet needs for people with dementia during their day include: memory support, access to information on support and care, social contact and company, and monitoring of health and perceived safety (to reduce anxiety) (cf. [1, 2]). Additionally, during night time, people with dementia can become disorientated when awakening leading to a range of problems including moving around inside and outside of their home, becoming emotional and reacting aggressively to situations. The causes are manifold but may be exacerbated by excessive day time sleeping, and night time incomprehension of time and place. Self-confidence and emotional wellbeing may be eroded in such circumstances leading to poor mental health and wellbeing overall (cf. [3]). In both day time and night time care of people with dementia, the role of the informal caregivers is critically important.

SenseCare aims to gather activity and related sensor data to infer the emotional state of the person with dementia as a knowledge stream of emotional signals. This interpretation is of value to three clear stakeholder groups. Firstly, the person with dementia whose wellbeing can be bolstered by the objective assessments of emotional wellbeing provided by the platform. This can reduce their anxiety and address key unmet needs such as access to information on their condition and care. Secondly, the informal family and friend care giver, can reflect on temporal trends in emotional assessment and state, and use the platform as an 'emotional wellbeing dashboard' to help guide their interventions. Thirdly, the primary care professionals, where the greater understanding of the emotional wellbeing of the person with dementia can be better understood with the insights available from the platform.

A key objective for the SenseCare platform is to provide a dashboard based visualisation of the emotional state of the people with dementia at home; based on inferring this state from emotional signals over time in multiple heterogeneous, high volume data streams. Such an interface requires significant effort to reduce the cognitive processing needed to interpret the information being visualised (cf. [4]). While different methods of visualisation of data for ambient assisted living services have been developed, these include more traditional visualisations of living spaces and activities over time, based primarily on inferring activities of daily living from activity sensor analysis (cf. [5]).

To introduce our approach of emotional state visualisation, we will first introduce general application scenarios that we would like to address within the SenseCare project. We than give a technical overview on the SenseCare platform and how we address the processing of the voluminous data streams on basis of the recently introduced Information Visualisation for Big Data (IVIS4BigData, cf. [25]) model, elaborate on the kind of data streams we would like to visualise and introduce our visualisation approach.

2 Application Scenarios and Relation to the SenseCare Platform

Within the SenseCare project we have identified three superordinate application scenarios. That is:

- *Assisted Living Scenario:* is dealing with people with dementia at home and their daily condition, where care giving practice can be finessed by monitoring of wellbeing and health conditions.
- *Emotional Monitoring Scenario:* is dealing with emotional monitoring of people with dementia during medical treatment to enable healthcare personnel to lessen false/positive rates during treatment sessions. False/positive rates are wrong conclusion rates of therapists done by misinterpretation of the emotional signals from the person with dementia. By having emotional monitoring in place during visits, the healthcare professionals are able to judge behaviour of people with dementia in an improved and more informed way. In this scenario SenseCare can be understood as a tool for healthcare professionals in order to raise therapy quality.
- *Shared care giving Scenario*: is dealing with requirements that come into existence if a group of people are involved in a treatment. During treatment processes several groups of persons and actions are generating data. To enable caregivers to have a clear picture of the condition and history of the person with dementia, data needs to be archived in searchable, accessible, visualisable and human readable ways. The goal is that the collection of information enables stakeholders to provide better wellbeing towards the person with dementia and to improve therapies with additional diagnostic information.

One example for the Shared Care giving scenario could be as follows: Sonia is female and 60 years of age. She has dementia and lives on her own. She gets frequent phone calls from family members and often receives a call from her nephew Ben. The SenseCare platform has computed that Sonia's emotional wellbeing has been declining over the past week and the carer has been notified of this. The carer logs onto the dashboard and observes some trends. It highlights that Sonia's positive emotions peak during a periodic phone call she receives once a month on a Tuesday afternoon.

The carer visits Sonia and carries out a mental health assessment. Sonia's health seems to be fine but after gaining permission, the carer phones Ben to reinforce that his phone calls have a positive effect on Sonia's emotional wellbeing and he is encouraged to phone more often, perhaps weekly. Ben is delighted to be notified of this and calls

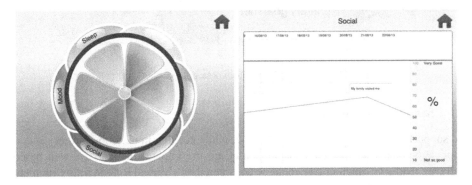

Fig. 1. Overview feedback wheel and Graph data for a person's self-reported quality of social interactions from (cf. [7])

Sonia once a week. A few months later, the SenseCare platform shows that this weekly phone call has had a significant effect on Sonia's emotional wellbeing.

How will emotional signals be stored, how will they be provided to the user and which emotional signals would be visualised? Research in this area has focused on derived features from sensor data correlated to measures of "anxiety, sleep quality, depression, loneliness, cognition, quality of life and independent living skills" (cf. [6]). This work has been further developed to provide visualisations that incorporate a holistic perspective on the wellbeing of an older person living independently including emotional aspects of their wellbeing (cf. Fig. 1 and [7]).

Other work adopts strong metaphorical perspectives to help visualise activities, in this case daily exercise (cf. Fig. 2 and [8]). In this work, the ambition was to produce a glanceable display, using a "stylized, aesthetic representation of physical activities and goal attainment to keep the individual focused on the act of self-monitoring and her commitment to fitness." In this representation, different types of flowers represent activities encompassing cardiovascular training, strength training, flexibility training, walking as well as activities such as housework or chopping wood. Each flower represents an individual event, for example, "a 40-minute run and a 3-hour bicycle ride are each represented by one pink cardio flower, etc. In order to get a better understanding of our visualisation approach in such application scenarios in SenseCare, we now present an overview of the Platform itself and the signals processed.

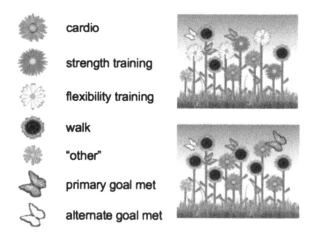

Fig. 2. Garden mappings and two sample gardens (cf. [8])

2.1 SenseCare Platform

To support this use case described in Sect. 2, while keeping in mind the further general application scenarios, we envision in SenseCare the implementation of a web based software platform which in fact could be considered as a Virtual Research Environment that facilitates the analysis, management and shared observation of affective data resources between the various involved stakeholders.

We will build upon a four layered software architecture (cf. Fig. 3). The topmost layer is the Application Layer that specifies the application scenarios for the SenseCare Platform. Beneath, the Service Layer integrates all services that are required to manage and process sensor data for its later comprehensive access and visualisation. Within this layer we distinguish two main responsibilities: On the one hand the management of sensory data, that will be realised through the so-called "Ecosystem Portal" (EP, cf. [26]) tool suite that was implemented by the software company GLOBIT. The EP tool suite was developed as a solution for the growing need of scientific communities to manage their document and media collections as well as their educational and other kinds of knowledge resources" (cf. [9]). The EP is a flexible software solution that is built around the content management functionality provided by the Typo3 framework. The modular setup of Typo3 allows the easy extension of functionality through the implementation of individual plugins. Within the runtime of the project we expect to provide EP plugins with interfaces for various kinds of sensor data. On the other hand, sensory data has to be searchable and manageable across the usage scenarios and their processes.

To address these requirements a Patient Data Management (PDM) systems will be developed, in fact this will be applied to handle the expected fast increasing data collection (cf. [20]). While working with processes the sensory archive with its information lifecycle for archive systems (cf. [21]) will be supplemented with sensory data lifecycles and its management system in the style of Product Data Management systems in order to establish collaborative processes (cf. [22]) in a Patient Data Life-cycle Management (PDLM) system. Next to data archive and management fields we will focus on the analysis and fusion of managed data which is computational expensive due to the complexity of the sensory data streams. For example, at any one moment the sensory processing adaptors may have to deal with varying sensory data input types such as facial video, physiological signals and perhaps audio frequencies. In isolation, each set of sensory data provides specific features be they video, physiological or frequency based. To perfect the analytical confidence in the emotional and cognitive sensory signals, the unification process (combination of multi-sensor based affective data streams) within the sensory fusion processing layer of SenseCare will also have to deal with the selection, integration, harmonisation, noise cancellation and quality assurance of the various sensory feature vectors that relate to the emotional state of the person with dementia in near real-time. Today such computationally intensive and expensive functionality can now be realised via infrastructure such as cloud based big data services. Therefore, we will provide a Big Data Service stack that enables the configuration of analysis workflows, to combine various services like Data Filtering, Machine Learning or Quality Assurance. In fact, the services and resources will be transferred and executed within the lowermost Infrastructure Layer to enable efficient analysis of provided data resources.

Actually, we decided to diminish a further Resource Layer between the Service and the Infrastructure Layer that specifies all applied data resources and adapters for further processing.

The introduced architecture provides just a technical overview about the components that constitutes the SenseCare Portal, but does not specify the interaction between the components, provided data and the portal users itself. However, these interactions

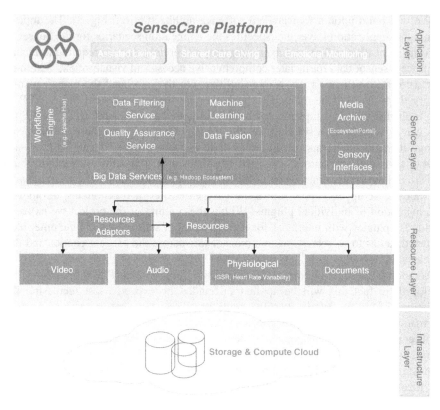

Fig. 3. SenseCare platform architecture

could be specified by means of the so called IVIS4BigData Model (cf. [25] and Fig. 4), that consists out of various interacting layers.

In the first *Data Collection, Management & Curation* layer, the captured emotion signals are managed within the portal Media Archive, that in fact make use of the previously introduced PDLM System in order to manage the dynamic nature of provided data. Within the next IVIS4BigData *Analytics* layer, the subset of required data is transformed into a Big Data Storage Technology compatible format (as e.g. HDFS), to be ready for Big Data analytics (provided in our Big Data Stack). In fact, this step already is a transformation action that leads to the first step within the IVIS4BigData *Interaction & Perception* layer and as such prepares the input for the Visual Mapping step that refines the available data for further processing with respect to the generation of Visual Structures, used for producing portal user views.

However, the *Insight and Effectuation* layer denotes to the user of the SenseCare Portal who interact with these views to satisfy his specific information needs either to gain just an overview of the provided data or to create knew knowledge from the provided information.

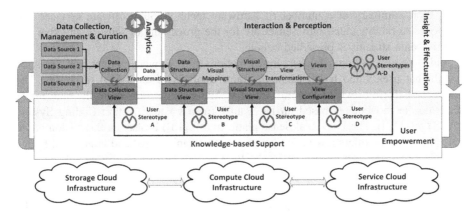

Fig. 4. IVIS4BigData Model (cf. [25])

Indeed, such newly created knowledge should be again collected, enriched with further information and managed through the portal and its components. Hence, all information that has been generated through the interaction of users with portal views could again influence all the previously mentioned layers of the IVIS4BIgData model.

2.2 Emotion Signals (Data Streams)

With reference to the SenseCare platform described above, the work of van den Broek (cf. [10]) in his paper Ubiquitous Emotion-Aware Computing focuses on interface advances over the past number of year. Today sub-domains of computer science such as ambient intelligence (AmI); pervasive computing; wearable computing; haptic computing and things that think (Internet of Things) are every day topics of leading scientific research. A key tenet of van den Broek's research is that the true potential of these fields will only be realised if human behaviour can also be analysed automatically. SenseCare is interrelated with all of the fields that van den Broek discusses with automatic analysis of behaviour and emotional/cognitive states at the heart of the SenseCare project.

As Picard outlines in her original publication Affective Computing (cf. [11]) emotional cues can be automatically garnered in many ways. Facial expressions, voice intonation, gestures, body movement/language, posture and pupillary dilation are all indicators that are easily apparent and can be read by humans and ever increasingly by machines. Emotional state is also present but certainly less apparent when physiological indicators such as respiration, heart rate, pulse, temperature, electrodermal response (skin), perspiration, muscle action potentials, blood pressure (Picard, 1997, pg. 27) and brain signals (electroencephalogram (EEG)) are integrated into the emotion analytical process. Today wearable computing and Internet of Things (IoTs) developments have truly opened up the potential to tap into these less apparent emotional and cognitive cues.

A short summary of a number of hardware technologies, software services and techniques to be integrated into SenseCare for the processing of sensory affective and cognitive data streams is presented below.

Video based emotional data streams: Emotient (http://www.emotient.com/) provide an API that uses video based frame-by-frame analysis of emotional responses. The Emotient platform provides data on 19 Facial Action Units, which are the elementary facial muscle movements based on Dr. Paul Ekman's Facial Action Coding System (FACS) (cf. [12]). The Intel Real Sense platform (cf. [13]) is also another vision based SDK platform that offers raw vision based data that can be used and interpreted by the SenseCare platform. Up to early 2016, the Real Sense platform also provided access to a partial set of the Emotient algorithms. Apple's recent purchase of Emotient has seen the removal of affect recognition from the Real Sense platform. At present, Apple's plans for Emotient are unclear and it remains to be seen if Apple will open up the Emotient platform to researchers and developers. Affectiva (cf. [14]) also provide vision based emotion analytics and claims to have processed almost four million facial images using their AI based platform. SenseCare will be designed to interface with vision based emotional analytical platforms similar to those discussed above.

Wearable based emotional data streams: Shimmer is an established provider of sensory physiological computing for affect recognition using GSR (Galvanic Skin Response), ECG (ElectroCardioGram) and EMG (ElectroMyoGram) (cf. [15]). Empatica has its origins in the affective sciences and specialises in clinical grade wearables. Their research focused E4 wrist worn device provides embedded sensors for photoplethysmography (PPG for continuous hearth rate analytics), electrodermal activity (EDA analytics for galvanic skin response, sympathetic activation, autonomic arousal and excitement), a 3-axis accelerometer for movement data and an infrared skin temperature thermopile. The Empatica Connect cloud service provides access to encrypted data, CSV format downloads, and precise time stamped data and signal comparison data services (cf. [16]. SenseCare architecture will also be designed to interface with wearables and IoTs based emotional analytical services and platforms similar to those described above.

Other sources of emotional data streams: There are ever increasing sources of affective data streams emerging from academic laboratories and reaching real-world application status. Voice emotion analytics (cf. [17]), EEG signal processing (cf. [18]), affective gait analytics (cf. [19]) are also expected to be future sensory fusion interface candidates for inclusion in the next iterations of the SenseCare platform.

Fusion of emotional data streams: One of the core competencies of the SenseCare partnership is the knowledge and expertise in the processing and fusion of sensory signals, data filtering and applied machine learning. SenseCare is being designed to incorporate a suite of affective sensory adaptors that enable access to recognized and open source APIs and SDKs in the field. The resulting domain related (dementia care in the case of SenseCare) multi-sensory based affective and cognitive intelligence will be the result of the sensory fusion process and various applied algorithms that will form the computational core of the SenseCare platform.

3   Visualisation of Emotion Signals

An interactive visualisation model will be implemented to allow authorized users to interrogate the various kind of streaming data, that we have described in Sect. 2.2, at 'different levels of detail'. The highest level will likely incorporate radar plots to visualise the frequency of emotions with reference to two baselines (a personal baseline [the normal frequency of each emotion for that individual] and a peer baseline [the mean frequency of each emotion as derived from all participants using the SenseCare platform]). A colour scheme similar to a traffic-lights approach will be taken to provide an effective visual hierarchy (making critical information unavoidable to the human visual system). Temporal visualisations will be used to depict the change in emotions over time, which will indicate days and times when participants are most vulnerable as well as indicating any correlations or patterns between affective states and activities (e.g. visitations and TV episodes etc.). Spatial visualisations will also overlay patterns in emotions and the participant's geo-locations. The novelty will involve the semantic search-ability of the data in the dashboard and the ability for data exploration and interrogation at multiple levels. All visualisations will be co-created with participants and will be underpinned by principles taken from cognitive and Gestalt psychology as well as human factors research.

3.1   Birthing Affectography and the Affectogram

Visualising emotions and in particular emotional wellbeing is a key research challenge. For such a visualisation to be adopted, it would need to be effective, standardized and well accepted using an intuitive metaphor. Moreover, this goal is significant given that medical visualisations in healthcare are often standardized to allow for consistent and universal diagnostic interpretations and training worldwide. For example, a cardiologist is known to interpret a standard presentation of the electrocardiogram (ECG) regardless of their jurisdiction or training. The same can be said for the radiologist who interprets standard presentations of X-rays and other radiographic images. With this in mind, it would be helpful for a psychiatrist to have the facility to interpret a standard visualisation of a person's emotional wellbeing and perhaps this would be the birth of affectography and the affectogram (AGM). Since Drake et al. [23] identified issues with Moodscope's AGM, the conception of a standard AGM remains a research challenge with an opportunity to contribute to better diagnostics in psychiatry and psychology. In conceiving the SenseCare framework [24], we have prototyped a number of AGMs. Figure 5 is one example of a potential AGM which we are proposing. Figure 5 is a visualisation based on the circumflex model of affect, which is a spatial schematic that allows any emotion to be plotted.

In our example, we use a heat map to visualise the frequency of emotions for an individual over a specific time period (this is often referred to as a spatiotemporal visualisation and is often used in medicine such as EEG). In the plot, the colour red would indicate the most frequent affective states whereas the colour blue indicates the least affective states. In this example, we also provide two indices, one which indicates the emotional well-being of the person and one which indicates the reliability of the

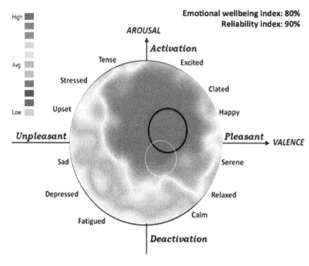

21st June 2016 - 21st July 2016

Fig. 5. A working prototype towards a standard affectogram

visualisation. The emotional wellbeing index could be calculated as such: Emotional wellbeing index = (good emotions/all emotions × reliability) × 100. Moreover, the reliability metric would be linked to the integrity of the sensor that is used to infer certain emotions and the reliability of the sampling. The circles in this example would depict a population based benchmark and a personalised benchmark or goal. Whilst this visualisation has a number of limitations (especially for showing temporal trends and patterns), it is a working prototype that could lead to standardising the first AGM.

The affectogram visualisation will be instantiated using an underlying common data structure such as EmotionML. However, organising the emotions into such a format will require pre-processing to harmonise all emotion classifications that are detected using each of the different modalities (i.e. audio, video, wearable). The ambition of this visualisation framework is to provide a standard affectogram and a standard underlying digital storage format that are modality independent. This would allow our affectogram to be used by many researchers and institutions regardless of how they detect human emotions.

4   Future Work

Based on the functional and non-functional requirements that results from identified frame conditions, we will setup a conceptual model of the SenseCare platform and harmonize and implement the identified software components. Finally, we will integrate these, to build the SenseCare platform. Throughout the project, people with early dementia and carers will be recruited and form the focus group to evaluate the concept, design and prototypes. The ethics has been approved by Ulster University, UK.

Through different pilot applications, with test data from our project partners, we then expect to refine iteratively the functionality of our platform. As SenseCare is a research project in a preclinical phase with no direct engagement with people with dementia–rather the system will be evaluated initially by healthcare specialists by trialing of the software tools using agile methodologies. After deployment the system will be validated in a formal healthcare evaluation phase, which will be done outside the scope of this project.

Acknowledgement. This publication has been produced in the context of the SenseCare project. This project has received funding from the European Union's H2020 Programme under grant agreement No. 690862. However, this paper reflects only the author's view and the European Commission is not responsible for any use that may be made of the information it contains.

References

1. Meiland, F., Davies, R., Moelaert, F., Mulvenna, M.D., Nugent, C., Dröes, R.-M.: Review of ICT-based services for identified unmet needs in people with dementia. Ageing Res. Rev. **6**(3), 223–246 (2007)
2. Walters, K., Iliffe, S., See Tai, S., Orrell, M.: Assessing needs from patient, carer and professional perspectives: the Camberwell assessment of need for the elderly people in primary care. Age Ageing **29**, 505–510 (2000)
3. Carswell, W., McCullagh, P., Augusto, J.C., Martin, S., Mulvenna, M.D., Zheng, H., Wang, H.Y., Wallace, J.G., McSorley, K., Taylor, B., Jeffers, P.: A review of the role of assistive technology for people with dementia in the hours of darkness. Technol. Health Care **17**(4), 281–304 (2009)
4. Takacs, B., Hanak, D.: A mobile system for assisted living with ambient facial interfaces. Int. J. Comput. Sci. Inf. Syst. **2**(2), 33–50 (2007)
5. Mulvenna, M.D., Carswell, W., McCullagh, P.J., Augusto, J.C., Zheng, H., Jeffers, P., Wang, H.Y., Martin, S.: Visualization of data for ambient assisted living services. IEEE Commun. Mag. **49**(1), 110–117 (2011)
6. Walsh, L., Kealy, A., Loane, J., Doyle J., and Bond, R.: Inferring health metrics from ambient smart home data. In: IEEE International Conference on Bioinformatics and Biomedicine (BIBM), Belfast, pp. 27–32 (2014)
7. Doyle, J., Walsh, L., Sassu, A., McDonagh. T.: Designing a wellness self-management tool for older adults: results from a field trial of YourWellness. In: Proceedings of the 8th International Conference on Pervasive Computing Technologies for Healthcare, pp. 134–141 (2014)
8. Consolvo, S., Klasnja, P., McDonald, D.W., Avrahami, D., Froehlich, J., LeGrand, L., Libby, R., Mosher, K., Landay. J.A.: Flowers or a robot army? Encouraging awareness & activity with personal, mobile displays. In: Proceedings of the 10th International Conference on Ubiquitous Computing (UbiComp 2008), pp. 54–63. ACM, New York (2008)
9. Nawroth, C., Schmedding, M., Brocks, H., Kaufmann, M., Fuchs, M., Hemmje, M.: Towards cloud-based knowledge capturing based on natural language processing. Procedia Comput. Sci. **68**, 206–216 (2015)
10. van den Broek, E.: Ubiquitous emotion-aware computing. Personal. Ubiquit. Comput. **17**(1), 53–67 (2013)

11. Picard, R.: Affective Computing. MIT Press, Cambridge (1997)
12. Emotient: Emotient API (2014). http://www.emotient.com/products#FACETSDK. Accessed 12 Sep 2014
13. Intel Real Sense: Real Sense Architecture (2014). https://software.intel.com/sites/landingpage/perceptual_computing/documentation/html/. Accessed 30 Apr 2014
14. Affectiva: Affdex (2015). http://www.affectiva.com/affdex/#pane_overview. Accessed 07 May 2015
15. Shimmer: Shimmer Sensing (2014). http://www.shimmersensing.com/. Accessed 17 Apr 2014
16. Empatica: E4 Wristband (2015). https://www.empatica.com/product-e4. Accessed 17 Apr 2015
17. Schuller, B., Eyben, F., Weninger, F.: OpenAudio, 09 March 2016. http://www.openaudio.eu/. Accessed 09 Mar 2016
18. Emotiv: Emotiv EPOC, 05 February 2015. http://emotiv.com/. Accessed 05 Feb 2015
19. PSFK.COM: Kinect system reads emotions to help autistic children socialize (2014). http://www.psfk.com/2014/03/kinect-autism-emotion-detection.html#!D1LyT. Accessed 17 Apr 2014
20. Metnitz, P.G.H., Lenz, K.: Patient data management systems in intensive care – the situation in Europe. Intense Care Med. 21(9), 703–715 (1995). ISSN: 1432-1238. Springer
21. Brooks, H., Kranstedt, A., Jäschke, G., Hemmje, M.: Modeling context for digital preservation. Stud. Comput. Intell. 260, 197–226 (2010)
22. Ming, X.G., Yan, J.Q., Wang, X.H., Li, S.N., Lu, W.F., Peng, Q.J., Ma, Y.S.: Collaborative process planning and manufacturing in product lifecycle management. Comput. Ind. 59(2–3), 154–166 (2008)
23. Drake, G., Csipke, E., Wykes, T.: Assessing your mood online: acceptability and use of Moodscope. Psychol. Med. 7(7), 1455–1464 (2013)
24. Bond, R.R., Zheng, H, Wang, H.Y., Mulvenna, M.D., McAllister, P., Delaney, K., Wlash, P., Keary, A., Riestra, R., Guaylupo, S., Hemmje, M., Becker, J., Engel, F.: SenseCare: using affective computing to manage and care for the emotional wellbeing of older people. In: EAI International Conference on Wearables in Healthcare (HealthWear), Budapest, 14–15 June 2016
25. Bornschlegl, M.X., Berwind, K., Kaufmann, M., Engel, F.C., Walsh, P., Hemmje, M.L.: IVIS4BigData: a reference model for advanced visual interfaces supporting big data analysis in virtual research environments. In: Proceedings of IVIS4BigData: A Reference Model for Advanced Visual Interfaces Supporting Big Data Analysis in Virtual Research Environments (2016)

Toward Interactive Visualization of Results from Domain-Specific Text Analytics

Tobias Swoboda[1]([✉]), Christian Nawroth[1], Michael Kaufmann[2],
and Matthias L. Hemmje[1]

[1] Faculty of Mathematics and Computer Science, University of Hagen,
Universitätsstraße 47, 58085 Hagen, Germany
{Tobias.Swoboda,Christian.Nawroth,Matthias.Hemmje}@fernuni-hagen.de
[2] School of Engineering and Architecture, Lucerne University of Applied Sciences
and Arts, Technikumstrasse 21, 6048 Horw, Switzerland
m.kaufmann@hslu.ch

Abstract. In big data analytics, visualization and access are central for the creation of knowledge and value from data. Interactive visualizations of analysis of structured data are commonplace. In this paper, information visualization and interaction for text analysis are addressed. The paper motivates this issue from a data usage standpoint, gives a survey of approaches in the area of interactive visualization of text analytics, and presents our proposal of a specific solution design for visual interaction with results from a combination of named entity recognition (NER) and text categorization (TC). This matrix-based model illustrates abstract views on complex relationships between abstract entities and is exemplary for any combination of feature extraction and TC. The aim of our proposal is to support feature extraction and TC researchers in distributed virtual research environments by providing intuitive visual interfaces.

Keywords: Interactive visualization · Text analysis

1 Introduction and Motivation

Interactive visualization is an important aspect of data analysis because this is the part of the process where human decision makers are confronted with the analysis results and, thus, where the transformation of data to knowledge takes place (a data-to-knowledge interface). According to the NIST big data reference architecture [17] visualization is on top of both the information and IT value chain. Kaufmann [12] suggests that interaction with data is central to value creation from big data. Thus, visualization provides the most value to the data consumer. Bornschlegl et al. [4] propose to incorporate information visualization as a central layer for big data management. Based on this general approach, we propose to apply interactive visualization techniques to text analytics in general and present a specific method as an example.

© Springer International Publishing AG 2016
M.X. Bornschlegl et al. (Eds.): AVI-BDA 2016, LNCS 10084, pp. 75–87, 2016.
DOI: 10.1007/978-3-319-50070-6_6

Researchers cooperate globally in virtual research environments (VREs) [5]. Among other features, these are web-based and allow for sharing intermediate and final research results. The research performed in these environments is becoming increasingly interdisciplinary, thus making the finding of possible source material more challenging. Certain problems have possibly already been solved in another branch of science, yet finding this solution, which has possibly been described in a different technical vocabulary, is not trivial for researchers from another field. The scientific publication rate has steadily increased, while the amount of coverage in literature databases, such as the Science Citation Index (SCI) and Social Sciences Citation Index (SSCI), has not kept up [13]. This means that finding the required knowledge resources to further one's research can become highly time consuming, which is not always a successful task. To alleviate this problem, text categorization (TC) can be used. Text categorization is the undertaking of assigning unstructured texts to a set of predefined categories [18]. As categories are also commonly referred to as classes, the problem is also known as classification and the systems performing TC as classifiers. Knowledge domain-specific, possibly hierarchical, category sets (also known as taxonomies) can be used. If a digital library, as part of a VRE, automatically assigns published documents to several knowledge organization schemes, researchers with different backgrounds can benefit.

In big data, the data that is worked with can be characterized by the following five criteria [8]: The *volume* of data as the scope is immense; the *velocity* of data as it is constantly generated and updated; the *variety* of data because it is largely heterogeneous; there is *veracity* of data because not everything that is processed is necessarily correct; and lastly that there is *value* to be yielded from the data. Attempting to perform manual text categorization (TC) in such an environment is a prohibitively time-consuming task. To overcome this challenge, there are different natural language processing (NLP)-based techniques to automate the process. A commonly used family of techniques is based on machine learning. Many machine-learning techniques for TC work on high-dimensional numerical representations of the document instead of the text itself. There are also a variety of techniques to derive these numerical representations, commonly referred to as feature extraction techniques. Bag of words (BOW) and named entity recognition (NER) are a few examples of such techniques. This paper investigates the state of the art and outlines our approach in visualizing such high-dimensional representations in order to facilitate their manipulation to optimize the overall text categorization effectiveness. Albeit these techniques are also usable on smaller text categorization use-cases, the sheer amount of heterogeneous fast-moving textual data in the publicly accessible internet alone makes it a big data topic.

Our research challenge is to visualize combinations of NER entities and TC-categories. Besides the research into TC itself, these techniques can also benefit researchers using VREs, as new publications in the digital library can be found by using this visual interface to identify NERs and found TC categories for all existing and new documents. In [16] we discussed our ideas on combining named entity recognition (NER) and support vector machine (SVM)-based TC in a domain-specific information retrieval (IR) system as part of an overall environment called AGNERS in the EU research project RAGE. In this system design, three use cases are being implemented: (1) related entity finding [1], (2) faceted search and (3) traditional keyword search. The facets in the search interface are filled with filter keywords based on an SVM-based text categorization. The input vectors for the SVMs are based on NER. This research investigates whether domain-specific NER combined with SVM-based categorization are a suitable concept for supporting the faceted search of end users. For this research, it is necessary to identify the correlation between identified named entity concepts in the corpus and document categorizations by the SVM.

The aim of our proposed visualization is the interactive visualization of these correlations. We think that interactive visualizations provide added value to the analysis because the NLP/IR researcher can more easily grasp correlations in visual representation. The benefit of this system is that the NLP/IR researcher can adapt and improve the NER as well as the classifier performance based on the visual insights. Referring to the NIST reference architecture, this means that the data consumer in our visualization project is not the end user but, as indicated, the NLP/IR researcher. In our vision, the NLP/IR researcher can identify multiple aspects of NER-based text classification:

– Biased Classification: Clusters of classification can be identified. Are there just a few classes in which texts are categorized or is there an equal distribution visible?
– Evaluate the taxonomy on the NER as well as on the text categorization side: Are there NER concepts that have no influence on the classification results? Are there text classes that are not filled by the classifier?
– Lookup of classification failure: If a text category is identified in which obviously texts are categorized by mistake, related NER concepts that have led to the classification failure can be identified.

We provide examples for these points in Sect. 3. In the following, in Sect. 2 we conduct a short survey on existing methods for interactive visualizations of text analytics; in Sect. 3 we present our model for a specific interactive visualization in an NLP research context; in Sect. 4 we evaluate our proposed system using referenced architectures introduced previously; and in Sect. 5 we conclude with a discussion and some suggestions for further research.

2   State-of-the-Art and Related Work

The automation of TC frees up the sparse time of domain experts for other tasks and actually enables TC for big data in the first place. There are two fundamental approaches for text categorization. The first is the usage of predefined rules that check for the appearance of certain keywords in the text in order to assign it to a category. The other basic method is machine learning. Based on Mohri et al. [15], machine learning can be summarized as computational methods that use past experience to make accurate predictions. Following Singh and Reddy's review of big data platforms [19], common machine-learning environments for big data applications are based on the in-memory computing environment, Spark, and the machine learning library, MLib [14]. Both were originally parts of the Berkeley Data Analysis Stack. As described in [18, 21], text categorization can be broken down into multiple phases. The first phase extracts feature vectors from the documents. The second phase selects the features that are most useful to identify the individual documents, while the third phase is the actual machine-learning-based text categorization. This is necessary because machine-learning methods usually work on numerical vector representations of the text and not directly on the text. There are a number of different approaches for deriving and selecting the feature vectors for TC.

Simply counting and then normalizing the occurrence of certain keywords is called the *bag of words* (BOW) method. A more advanced feature extraction method is *named entity recognition* (NER), the process of finding tokens within the text that can be identified as named representations or labels of certain concepts within the taxonomy. In standard NER typical concepts representing named entities are *location, person* and *organization* [11]. A simple example for NER is that the tokens *Bari, Lucerne* and *Hagen* can all be regarded as named entities of the class *location*. The relationship between named entities, target categories and the documents are therefore of high interest when attempting to optimize the overall performance.

Our proposed system can be regarded as applied knowledge management in an area, where the amount of generated data, information and knowledge prohibits an entirely manual approach. To manage applications such as this, Kaufmann introduced the *Big Data Management Meta Model* (BDMcube) [12]. This meta model analyzes the process of big data management into five distinct layers with a closed loop. Each of these layers has a technical and an organizational, domain or business perspective to it. While the domain perspective focuses on what is to be achieved, the technical perspective focuses on the technical implementation. The layers are data integration, data analytics, data interaction, data effectuation and data intelligence. The first four layers form a conceptional loop, while the last aspects essentially provide the knowledge management across these four steps. Data integration focuses on the data sources. It assesses the kind of data that is accessed and how this access is implemented technically. Data analytics focuses on the analytical techniques and technologies that are used in the pursuit of gaining insight. Data interaction focuses on the human computer interaction. Insight can only be gained by an expert interacting with the automated system. Therefore, a small loop between data analytics and data interaction is part of the model. Data effectuation focuses on beneficially applying the gained insights. It addresses the future usage of the information gained. Among other usages, it is reused in the data integration phase. Data intelligence combines these four aspects in an overall epistemic process. The semantic annotation of generated documents and therefore the discipline of TC are part of data intelligence (Fig. 1).

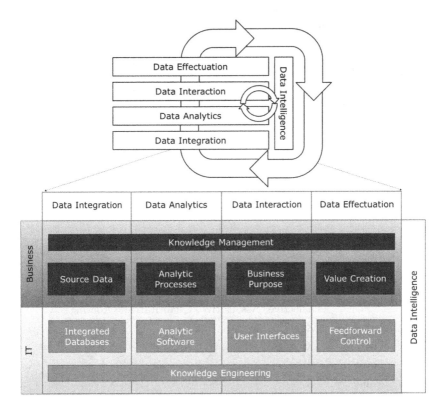

Fig. 1. BDMcube; Big Data Management Meta-Model (Kaufmann, 2016) [12]

Card et al. [6] introduced the Information Visualization (IVIS) Reference Model. Bornschlegl et al. extended the IVIS Reference Model as an instance of BDMcube toward the IVIS4BigData Reference Model [4]. At the core of IVIS and IVIS4BigData is the human interaction in the mapping processes of different views in the data. Views that can be consumed by human users are composed of visual structures. These are generated from data structures which in themselves are a product of data transformation from the source data.

Based on Bertin [2], there are a variety of visual attributes, each of which is suited for different aspects of human perception. These attributes are used in different visual elements used for visualization. The aspects of human perception are related to what aspects of the data one wishes to encode in the visual elements. These aspects, as shown in Table 1, are selective, associative, quantitative and ordering. *Selective* describes how well this attribute distinguishes a visual element from another. *Associative* describes how much a visual attribute influences the visibility of another. *Quantitative* describes how well numerical amounts can be encoded. *Ordering* indicates how well an ordering of data points can be conveyed using this visual attribute. The available attributes for visual elements are *location, size, form, alphanumeric value, color, orientation, texture*

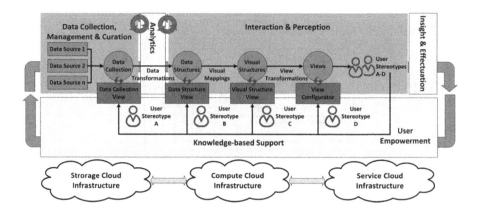

Fig. 2. IVIS4BigData reference model [4]

Table 1. Visual attributes for human perception [2]

	Selective	Associative	Quantitative	Ordering
Location	X	X	X	X
Size	X		X	X
Form		X		
Value	X			X
Color	X	X		
Orientation	X	X		
Texture	X	X		
Movement	X	X		

and *movement*. Table 1 maps the visual attributes to the different aspects of human perception. These attributes provide the fundamental vocabulary for any data visualization and thus the visual structures of the IVIS4BigData Reference Model (Fig. 2).

Several researchers have addressed the issue of interactive visualizations for text analytics. Grinstein et al. [10] compared a multitude of visualization techniques for high dimensional data points, suitable for visualizing results from text analytics. These include *scatter plots, heat maps, height maps, table lens, survey plots, dimensional stacking parallel coordinates, line graphs* and *polar charts*. Each of these techniques used a mix of the introduced visual attributes to visualize data. Chuang [7] introduced Termite, *"a visual analysis tool for assessing topic model quality"*. It is a matrix based visualization model that correlates terms and topics gained through a text corpus analysis. Other well-known interactive visualization systems for text analysis are *TIARA* by Wei et al. [22] and *LeadLine* by Dou et al. [9]. TIARA provides topic-based interactive visualization of large text collections, whereas LeadLine follows an approach to visualize events in text collections. *Jigsaw* [20] is a system that provides text analysis for law enforcement investigators and that supports several interactive visualizations for example graph based ones. The approaches mentioned above are content-based.

Other than these content-based visualization approaches, there also exist metadata-based alternatives. Due to the variety and veracity of big data, one cannot reliably presume that usable metadata is available. As we will show, our approach can be classified as a hybrid approach, as it depends neither on full text nor on native metadata. In fact the proposed system works with secondary data derived from the NER and SVM system.

3   Model

The system model shown in [16] has been refined and extended. It now contains a NLP/IR-research-visualization component. The novel component is to be used for visual analysis of two input dimensions: Extracted feature vectors and performed categorizations. As feature extraction implementation, NER vectors are provided by the NER subsystem and correlated with the categorization results of the classifier subsystem. In the AGNERs case, the classifier is implemented using an SVM.

Our visualization model is based on the Termite system [7]. The Termite system correlates two dimensions: (general) terms and topics. It is based on the Latent Dirichlet Allocation (LDA) Model [3]. For our visualization approach, we will modify the concept of Termite and follow a more domain-specific approach: instead of general terms, we will use domain-specific named entity categories. The topics in the Termite concept are replaced by the categories of the faceted search. The categories are provided by a domain-specific taxonomy that is currently under development. Currently, an SVM implementation is used as a classifier component.

3.1   Interaction Model

To ensure the proposed analytical benefits, the visualization component must provide a high degree of interaction for the data consumer. For this we basically follow the interactive components of the Termite system: drill down, filter and ranking, supported by the saliency measure. We propose to adapt the saliency measure introduced by Termite with regard to named entities and classifications. Thus, the saliency in our project is used to identify specific named entity classes that determine the classification of documents more strongly than other named entity classes (Fig. 3).

$$saliency(n) = P(n) * distinctiveness(n) \tag{1}$$

Similar to the original saliency measure approach, the distinctiveness of a named entity concept is the Kullback-Leibler divergence between the NER concept and the text category assigned by the SVM. We think that saliency is the

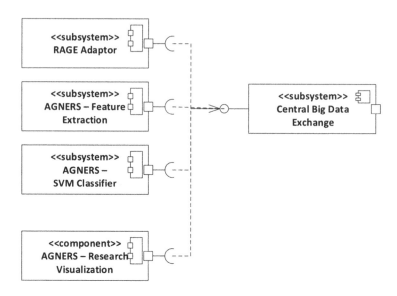

Fig. 3. The extended model based on the AGNERS IR in [16]

suitable filter and ranking criterion for the intended use case of investigating the correlations between named entities and classification results.

3.2   Visualization Model

The following wireframe shows how a matrix diagram can be used to visualize the correlation between examples of named entity classes and categories assigned by the SVM classifier. In our case, the named entity classes and categories are provided by a taxonomy that was developed during the AGNERS project and that is based on the existing state-of-the-art taxonomies of the applied gaming sector as well as requirements derived from the RAGE project [16]. Figure 4 provides an example of the visualization using a two-matrix display. The y-axis contains NER concepts, while the x-axis contains TC categories. In the example, there are four NER concepts: "government", "police", "military" and "automotive", as well as four text classes that are part of the taxonomy branch "target group": "army", "sportsmen", "lawyers" and "law enforcement". The circles indicate correlations between NER concepts and TC categories with circles whose sizes symbolize the number of documents in the classes.

In the example in Fig. 4, the following insights are possible: (A) Documents that contain the concepts "police" and "military" are categorized into the class "target group/sportsmen" (indicated by green circles). This categorization looks equally distributed and coherent regarding contents. (B) However, only documents containing the NER concept "police" are categorized into the class "target group/law enforcement". This may indicate a bias in this category, as there are, for example, other documents containing government and military concepts,

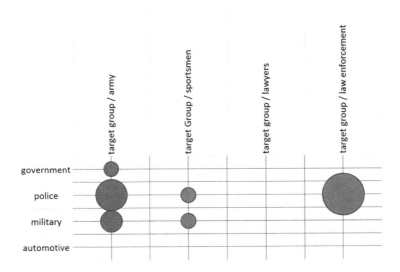

Fig. 4. Visual correlations between named entities and TC target classes (Color figure online)

which are also relevant for this target group. (C) Many documents containing the NER concept "police" are categorized into "target group/army". This could be an error. (D) The class "target group/lawyers" and the NER concept "automotive" are obviously not considered by the classifier. Again, this could indicate an area for improvement.

As indicated, drill-down is a specific feature of the proposed visual interaction. Drill-down allows the researcher to explore two additional dimensions of visualization:

NER concepts/Documents: This drill-down is shown in Fig. 5. In this dimension, the drill-down takes place at the x-axis of our visualization. By clicking a particular document category, all documents of this selected document category are displayed, and the according NER concepts in these documents are shown in the two-dimensional bubble view. This enables the researcher to discover the respective NER concepts that have been detected in the documents and, for example, to find false positive NER results.

NER concepts/Documents: This drill-down is shown in Fig. 6. In this case, a NER concept can be expanded, thus showing all documents containing the selected concept. The matrix then shows the assignment of these documents to the document categories. This allows the researcher to discover errors in the document categorization based on single documents.

Although the visualization remains two-dimensional, from a logical perspective our model covers more dimensions due to the drill-down functionality. It could thus be imagined as cube matching combinations of NER concepts, TC categories and actual documents. This could actually be used in the visualization

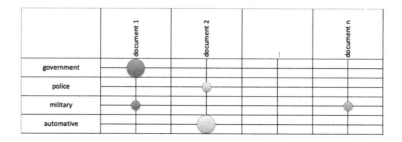

Fig. 5. Drilldown showing visual correlations between NER concepts and documents

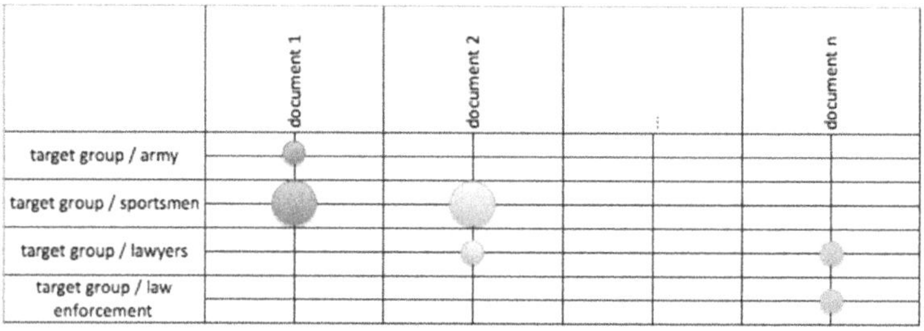

Fig. 6. Drilldown showing visual correlations between documents and categories

by actually rendering and rotating a three-dimensional cube of spheres on drill-downs. If e.g. a user drills down into the *NER concepts/Documents* view from the starting point of the *NER concepts/TC target classes* additional layers of spheres could be generated behind the presently displayed spheres. Then the whole cube can be turned. This way, unsers can keep the visual association with NER concepts in questions as they stay on the screen and simply move. After the rotation, the background spheres should be deleted to prevent cluttering of the visualization.

4 Discussion

When mapping our proposed system into BDMcube, the components are part of the inner loop between data analytics, data interaction and data intelligence. Data analytics occurs in the capture of the visualized data. Data interaction occurs with the interactive visual interface, while the domains of TC and NER in themselves are applied data intelligence. Deepening this view using IVIS4BigData, the analytics phase occurs in the collection and projection of extracted NEs and TC categories in a three-dimensional tensor, which provides our internal data structure. The utilized visual structures are matrices and spheres, while the overview and individual drill-downs provide different views. User interaction primarily occurs in the view transformation when selecting between different drill-downs. Insight and essentially effectuation occur in two ways. Firstly, new documents containing specific NEs or related to specific topics can be found using this visual interface and providing a new perspective on the available, rapidly growing document collection (e.g., in a VRE). Secondly, research into NER and TC can be aided by this visual feedback. Our approach also serves to improve Data Intelligence using knowledge extraction, because with the visualized form of interaction with keywords, users are better empowered to acquire knowledge from the document base. Our model addresses multiple big data challenges. Due to it's roots in Kaufmann's epestimological BDMcube it is focused on generating value from big data. This amount of natural language analysis is not manually possible because of the volume of documents in questions. It therefore addresses volume and velocity of data. Additionally, it enables the search for ill-fitting NER concepts and categories thus adressing veracity. Eventhough our approach focuses on the single data type of natural language, this datatype is highly unstructured and therefore a model focusing on veracity.

The usage of the visual attributes of location and size is well suited for human perception, as location ideally indicates the combination of elements such as NER concepts, TC concepts and documents, while the usage of size allows for an intuitional grasp of their correlation. Splitting up these steps into individual services makes them combinable with other services in a cloud environment, as envisioned in the IVIS4BigData reference model. A potential challenge in the implementation is a high amount of documents, categories and NER concepts. Not all are relevant for display and should therefore be filtered. The design of an interactive system that provides users with easy means to achieve this feat is certainly a challenge. The taxonomic aggregation of categories and NER concepts could help in this regard providing the means to zoom thus enabling focus and context.

5 Summary and Future Work

To summarize, we firstly motivated a more visual and interactive approach to text analytics with the NIST big data reference architecture and with the needs of NLP researchers in an ongoing research project; secondly, we have reviewed some existing literature on the subject; and, thirdly, we have presented a wireframe and an interactive visualization concept specifically for the combination of NER and TC. The insights provided can be used for fine tuning of the TC process, as proposed in the IVIS4BigData reference model, and as an instance of BDMcube providing a specific solution on how data interaction can help create value from big data. A simple and direct approach is to provide interactive aids to assign weights to the individual NER concepts and use them on the extracted feature vectors before passing them as arguments to the SVM-based classifier. There are several advantages of visually working with text analytics results, some of which we have discussed in the model section. Of course, the biggest drawback is the labor cost of implementation. Our model, at the current state, is only a concept, and there is no implementation and thus no evaluation possible so far.

To make evaluations possible, a working proof of concept is needed; only then can specific qualitative case studies and expert evaluations be presented. In the future, if the concept is received well by the community, we will implement a demonstrator for the proposed concept and perform qualitative evaluations with expert interviews to provide some insight on the usefulness into our information systems design.

References

1. Balog, K., Serdyukov, P., de Vries, A.P.: Overview of the TREC 2010 entity track. In: Proceedings of the Nineteenth Text REtrieval Conference (TREC). NIST (NIST Special Publication, SP 500–294) (2010)
2. Bertin, J.: Sémiologie Graphique, Editions Gauthier-Villars (1967). Paris, France (German translation Jensch, G., Schade, D., Scharfe, W. Graphische Semiologie. Diagramme Netze Karten Berlin (1974)
3. Blei, D.M., Ng, A.Y., Jordan, M.I., Lafferty, J.: Latent Dirichlet allocation. J. Mach. Learn. Res. **3**(45), 993–1022 (2003). doi:10.1162/jmlr.2003.3.4-5.993
4. Bornschlegl, M.X., Berwind, K., Kaufmann, M., Engel, F., Walsh, P., Hemmje, M.L., Riestra, R.: IVIS4BigData: a reference model for advanced visual interfaces supporting big data analysis in virtual research environments (2016)
5. Candela, L., Castelli, D., Pagano, P.: Virtual research environments: an overview and a research agenda. Data Sci. J. **12**, grdi75–grdi81 (2013). http://doi.org/10.2481/dsj.GRDI013
6. Card, S.K., Mackinlay, J.D., Shneiderman, B. (eds.): Readings in Information Visualization: Using Vision to Think. Morgan Kaufmann Publishers Inc., San Francisco (1999)
7. Chuang, J., Manning, C.D., Heer, J.: Termite: visualization techniques for assessing textual topic models. In: Proceedings of the International Working Conference on Advanced Visual Interfaces, pp. 74–77 (2012)
8. Demchenko, Y., Grosso, P., de Laat, C., Membrey, P.: Addressing big data issues in scientific data infrastructure. In: International Conference on Collaboration Technologies and Systems (CTS), p. 4855 (2013)
9. Dou, W., Wang, X., Skau, D., Ribarsky, W., Zhou, M.X.: LeadLine: interactive visual analysis of text data through event identification and exploration. In: IEEE Conference on Visual Analytics Science and Technology (VAST) (2012)
10. Grinstein, G., Trutschl, M., Cvek, U.: High Dimensional Visualization Institute for Visualization and Perception Research, University of Massachusetts Lowell (2001). http://www.cs.uml.edu/mtrutsch/research/High-Dimensional_Visualizations-KDD2001-color.pdf
11. Jurafsky, D., Martin, J.H.: Speech and language processing. In: An Introduction to Natural Language Processing, Computational Linguistics and Speech Recognition. Prentice Hall series in artificial intelligence, 2nd edn. Pearson Prentice Hall, Upper Saddle (2009)
12. Kaufmann, M.: Towards a reference model for big data management. Research report, Faculty of Mathematics, Computer Science, University of Hagen. https://ub-deposit.fernuni-hagen.de/receive/mir_mods_00000583. Accessed 4 July 2016
13. Larsen, P.O., Ins, M.: The rate of growth in scientific publication and the decline in coverage by science citation index. Scientometrics **84**(3), 575–603 (2010). Springer

14. MLib documentation. http://spark.apache.org/docs/latest/mllib-guide.html. Accessed 28 Feb
15. Mohri, M., Rostamizadeh, A., Talwalkar, A.: Foundations of Machine Learning. MIT Press, Cambridge (2012)
16. Nawroth, C., Schmedding, M., Brocks, H., Kaufmann, M., Fuchs, M., Hemmje, M.L.: Toward cloud-based knowledge capturing based on natural language processing. In: Machine Learning in Automated Text Categorization. HOLACONF - Cloud Forward: From Distributed to Complete Computing (2015)
17. NIST Special Publication 1500–6, NIST Big Data Interoperability Framework, vol. 6. Reference Architecture. http://nvlpubs.nist.gov/nistpubs/SpecialPublications/ NIST.Spp.1500-6.pdf. Accessed 7 Apr 2016
18. Sebastiani, F.: Machine learning in automated text categorization. ACM Comput. Surv. **34**, 1–47 (2002)
19. Singh, D., Reddy, C.K.: Survey on platforms for big data analytics. J. Big Data (2012). http://www.journalofbigdata.com/content/1/1/8. Accessed 28 Feb 2016
20. Stasko, J., Gärg, C., Liu, Z.: Jigsaw: supporting investigative analysis through interactive visualization. Inf. Vis. **7**(2), 118–132 (2008)
21. Swoboda, S., Kaufmann, M., Hemmje, M.L.: Toward cloud-based classification and annotation support. In: Proceedings of the 6th International Conference on Cloud Computing and Services Science (CLOSER 2016), vol. 2, pp. 131–137 (2016)
22. Wei, F., Liu, S., Song, Y., Pan, S., Zhou, M.X., Qian, W.: TIARA: a visual exploratory text analytic system. In: Proceedings of the 16th ACM SIGKDD International Conference on Knowledge Discovery and Data Mining, pp. 153–162 (2010)

Towards Synchronizing Data Sources and Information Visualization in Virtual Research Environments

Christian Danowski-Buhren[1(✉)], Marco X. Bornschlegl[1], Benno Schmidt[2], and Matthias L. Hemmje[1]

[1] University of Hagen, Hagen, Germany
christian.danowski@studium.fernuni-hagen.de,
{marco.bornschlegl,matthias.hemmje}@fernuni-hagen.de
[2] Bochum University of Applied Sciences, Bochum, Germany
benno.schmidt@hs-bochum.de

Abstract. There are many systems that visualize abstract data in the context of Information Visualization (IVIS). However, most systems create unidirectional visualizations that represent a static product of the source data. Possible changes to the content of the visualization – if that is possible at all – are not reflected to the data sources. This paper recommends a theoretical approach to use modern Web technologies and state-of-the-art system architectures to conceptualize a synchronization-enabled Web-based 3D IVIS infrastructure. Within applications built on top of this infrastructure, clients are able to modify data properties within three-dimensional real-time visualizations. In consequence, these content modifications are automatically transmitted to the server-side data sources for persistence. Moreover, relevant content changes on the server side are broadcast to all registered clients to maintain a permanent consistent state between data sources and derived IVIS-products. Particularly, a Mediator-Wrapper architecture is used in order to semantically integrate heterogeneous data sources in Big Data scenarios. Note that this paper presents a theoretical approach and that validation and evaluation are future tasks.

Keywords: 3D information visualization · Synchronization-enabled IVIS infrastructure · Mediator-Wrapper architecture · Big data

1 Introduction

Information Visualization (IVIS) constitutes the process of representing abstract data in a graphical way to support users in perceiving data properties and relations [21]. The *IVIS Reference Model* (also called *visualization pipeline*) depicts the necessary data structures (*Raw Data*, *Data Tables*, *Visual Structures* and *Views*) and transformations (*Data Transformations*, *Visual Mappings* and *View Transformations*) to produce cognitive efficient visual representations [8]. Via resulting views the user may interact with the displayed content.

In the context of *Big Data* scenarios in virtual research environments, Bornschlegl et al. [5] propose an extension of the *IVIS Reference Model* to conquer current challenges

M.X. Bornschlegl et al. (Eds.): AVI-BDA 2016, LNCS 10084, pp. 88–103, 2016.
DOI: 10.1007/978-3-319-50070-6_7

regarding data access, visualization, perception and interaction. Based on a *Mediator-Wrapper* architecture [29], they embed the elements of the *IVIS Reference Model* into the stages of Kaufmann's [17] *Big Data Management (BDM) Reference Model*, which provides a logical order of Big Data processes. Consequently, the resulting **IVIS4BigData Reference Model**, illustrated in Fig. 1, is capable of semantically integrating heterogeneous distributed data sources and use the distributed data content to create visual representations. Through these visual representations the core properties and relationships of the source data shall be explored and perceived by any human observer in a cognitive efficient manner [5]. To support this intuitive perception, *interactive 3D visualizations* are a promising solution. Each human being acts in 3D space in his everyday life. Thus, the usage of a virtual 3D depiction space for *IVIS* purposes seems obvious since a human observer is very familiar with the "control instructions" of such an environment.

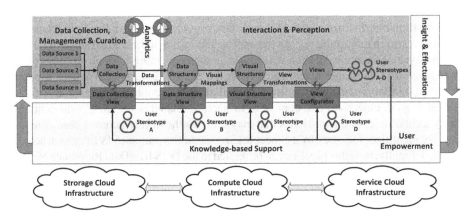

Fig. 1. IVIS4BigData Reference Model proposed by Bornschlegl et al. [5]

The World Wide Web (WWW) has evolved to be *the* interface for several aspects of daily life, e.g. applications in the fields of Social Media, communication and location-based services or information querying [7]. Keywords like "Web 2.0" or the "Participative Web" indicate that the role of application users shifts from passive consumers of services to active participants demanding for more empowerment with regard to content generation and modification as well as application interaction and configuration [19]. Considering users rising demands for content modification and creation, the *IVIS Reference Model* remains incomplete. Referring to the input of the visualization pipeline, the *Raw Data* component is more or less of static nature. A derived visualization represents a static product with respect to the displayed content. But what if the visualized content changes over time, e.g. due to dynamic data sources or user-initiated content modifications? Then previously derived visualizations do not reflect the most current state of content. Also, if users manipulate data properties within the visualizations, it would be aspirational to propagate these modifications back to the original data sources to make the changes persistent. To be precise, if necessary, users could apply updates to the actual data sources through the visual interface directly without the burden of switching applications or use an alternative data source access. The benefit of a bidirectional visualization pipeline is that users may not only view data and locally modify the view of certain source data, but are more importantly enabled to persist their modification of data instances by writing the modifications back to the concrete data sources. **In conclusion, the *IVIS Reference Model* is missing an explicit synchronization mechanism allowing content changes on both data source level and derived IVIS products, to maintain a synchronized and consistent state.**

This paper presents a theoretical approach to combine contemporary Web technologies and 3D real-time visualizations to establish a synchronization-enabled Web-based Big-Data-capable 3D IVIS infrastructure capable of synchronizing server-side data sources and (multiple) client-side information visualizations. Based on the *IVIS4BigData* Reference Model [5], the presented approach uses a generic *Mediator-Wrapper* architecture to integrate multiple heterogeneous data sources while offering a single uniform interface for clients [12] and, thus, provide support for Big Data scenarios in virtual research environments. As the approach is still in a theoretical stage of development, evaluation and validation will follow in the near future through a prototypical implementation. The paper is outlined as follows. Section 2 starts with a discussion of additional motivation and ends with the formulation of a problem statement as well as a research goal, objectives and approach. In Sect. 3, related work along with contemporary technologies and approaches that may serve as the infrastructure's base components are identified, followed by a conceptualization of the proposed IVIS infrastructure in Sect. 4. Finally, how this pipeline can be related to the IVIS4BigData Reference Model proposed by Bornschlegl et al. [5] is discussed in Sect. 5. An Overview of subsequent tasks concludes this paper.

2 Motivation, Problem Statement and Research Approach

This section discusses the need for a synchronization-enabled IVIS infrastructure from several perspectives, including the justification of a Web- and 3D interface as well as data-, user- and use-case-characteristics.

2.1 Justification of Web and 3D User Interface

Utilizing state-of-the-art Web technologies requires a permanent and preferably fast Internet connection as well as up-to-date browser versions from users. Despite these limitations, Web applications offer various advantages compared to desktop applications. The most important advantages are listed below and mainly taken from Chen and Heath [10] and Campesato and Nilson [7]:

- **Control over Application and Versioning:** the Web application can be easily modified as each client uses the most recent version from the server when he accesses the application.

- **Cross-Platform Capability:** a Web-based infrastructure is independent from a concrete Operating System. All that is required is an (up-to-date) Web browser that can run script code.
- **Access to Broad User Mass:** according to a German study the proportion of Internet users in Germany in 2015 was 77.6% [22]. Present society is very familiar with using Web interfaces and applications. In particular, Web applications may be accessed via different devices like classical personal computers/notebooks, tablets or even smartphones. Using latter devices even allows interaction with the application from nearly everywhere (as long as there is a stable Internet connection).
- **Enablement of Collaboration:** spatially disjoint users can be empowered to work collaboratively via the same Web interface.

The advantages of Web applications outweigh the disadvantages, as potential users from all over the world can be provided with a visual interface to a central data storage, allowing to interact with the data from anywhere. Hence, a Web-based infrastructure represents a powerful way to establish a synchronization-enabled IVIS application.

The choice of applying a 3D user interface should be discussed. Compared to a classical 2D interface, there are various advantages and disadvantages, as revealed and confirmed by a recent study performed by Dübel et al. [11]. In general, the main problem areas of a 3D visualization are perspective object distortion and occlusion as well as matching the spatial location of objects referring to the attribute space. In contrast to this, a comprehensive presentation of 3D spatial objects as well as an increased number of perceivable shapes are benefits [11]. With regard to the main IVIS intention, which is to support perception and insight of user by providing cognitive efficient and effective visualizations of abstract data [26], a third dimension might be utilized to map additional data properties to visual attributes [11].

However, designing an intuitive 3D user interface for IVIS applications is not trivial [9]. A successful 3D user interface has to consider the following five basic principles of Human-Computer Interaction (HCI), as presented by Ortega et al. [20]: *learnability, efficiency, memorability, low error rate* and *satisfaction*. If those basic principles are kept in mind, a 3D user interface for IVIS purposes built on contemporary 3D technologies could establish a powerful interface for exploring and perceiving abstract data.

2.2   Data Characteristics

The classical *IVIS Reference Model* was conceptualized for use cases with more or less static *Raw Data* as input for the visualization pipeline. User-triggered *Data Transformations* were intentionally considered to query raw data sources to select or filter content, which was used as input for the visualization processes, resulting in static visualization products with respect to the available content [8]. Considering the introduction of dynamic data sources and content, the *Raw Data* component of the *IVIS Reference Model* can be classified according to Table 1.

Table 1. Taxonomy of *Raw Data* in the *IVIS Reference Model* (static vs. dynamic *Raw Data*) – some arguments have been used from [16]

	Static *Raw Data*	Dynamic *Raw Data*
Content Modification	once created, **no modification**	**modification/removal** of existing content, **creation** of new content (**additional data**)
Accuracy/Fault Rate	**more reliable**, checked before release; usually **provided by domain experts**	**less reliable**, not necessarily checked; also **provided** by **participants without domain knowledge**
Data Sources	databases, data streams, file-based data, Web services with **static content;**	databases, data streams, file-based data, Web services **plus dynamically generated data** like sensor streams, simulation outputs **with dynamic content;**
Acquisition/Retrieval	select or filter operations **(querying and filtering)**	select or filter operations plus simulation output (**querying, filtering and simulating**)
Content Domain/Query Domain	**static** → query against **a priori known resources**	**dynamic** → query against **dynamic resources**, requires dynamic queries
Impact on Workflow of *IVIS Reference Model*	derived visualizations require **no update** due to static content	**synchronization** between content and derived visualizations needed maintenance of **consistency** between data sources and IVIS products

In essence, allowing *dynamic Raw Data* as basic component in the visualization pipeline has huge consequences for both the content of derived IVIS products and the workflow of the visualization pipeline. Moreover, as proposed by Bornschlegl et al. [5], the classical *IVIS Reference Model* should be extended to explicitly allow multiple heterogeneous data sources to match today's data landscape. A proposed extension is presented in Sect. 4.1.

2.3   User-Oriented Characteristics

The main intention of an IVIS application is to empower the user in analysing and perceiving data [8]. Typically, the user has a certain Information Need, executes appropriate Information Behaviour by interacting with the visualized content and eventually achieves insight. Hereby, the role of the IVIS application is to enhance the effectivity and efficiency of users' Human-Computer Interaction by reducing technical barriers [9]. The classical *IVIS Reference Model* offers several user-triggered interactions to request data and alter the visual outcome to iteratively analyse the data [26]. However, in addition, it would be beneficial to persist achieved insight within the original data sources and thus, make it public for other participants, as introduced in Sect. 1. In consequence, a modernized IVIS infrastructure should provide a *user-triggered update mechanism* to apply local data modifications to the original data sources. In order to keep data sources and visualizations consistent, any change at data source level must be immediately *broadcast* to all affected clients that visualize the changed content to maintain consistency. For instance, in a collaborative scenario, where researchers may analyse cancer genomic data [24], each researcher could persist his/her insight by pinning an annotation to a certain visual object. As this information is also persisted at the data source, it can be shared with all other researchers, who may benefit from it with regard to decision making and cognitive understanding.

2.4 Use Case Characteristics

There are many concrete use cases and scenarios, where the proposed IVIS infrastructure can be utilized. In particular, referring to virtual research environments, a concrete use case might be to establish an advanced visual interface to access and interact with relevant research content. In such an open research environment, several research parties may offer their data and services to others. If researchers browse the available content from different providers, they could use the visual interface to find relevant content and perform certain tasks, e.g. in the fields of data mining or visual analytics. Once the client-side visualization has been generated at a certain point in time, the server-side research content might change some time later. In this case, the derived visualization has to be notified and updated in order to reflect the most recent content inventory. More importantly, if researches want to modify or add their own data and services via the open research environment, they should be enabled to perform this directly through the visual interface. To be precise, based on an existing data model, researchers could modify existing or add new instances with a predefined data-structure through dedicated actions within the visual interface. These actions are, as a result, applied to the underlying data sources, where the new information is persisted. As soon as new information is available at data source level, all other researchers that currently visualize the affected datasets can be notified to retrieve it, thus, synchronizing their local visualization.

2.5 Problem Statement, Research Goal and -Objectives

To sum up the previous sections, the original *IVIS Reference Model* neglects the explicit intention to synchronize data sources and derived information visualizations. From the perspective of Web 2.0, where users shall be empowered to actively generate and interact with data, the lack of data modifiability in current IVIS Web applications is a deficit. Hence, suitable means for content modification as well as an explicit synchronization mechanism are aspirational to establish an extended visualization pipeline capable of synchronizing data sources and derived information visualizations. With respect to concrete Web-based IVIS infrastructures and applications, the following main Research Questions have to be considered:

- *are there existing visualization generation tools that consider cognitive efficient interactive means to modify and synchronize IVIS content during the generation process?* In other words, when a synchronization-enabled visualization is generated, suitable user interaction and modification mechanisms have to be inserted into the delivered visual product. This includes the question: *which formats allow these high-level interactions and modifications in the first place?*
- *during runtime, how can Web-based event-handling of 3D-visualization-embedded user interaction and modification tools be realized to allow users to (i) explore the displayed data, (ii) request additional data and (iii) modify data properties? How can relevant information be exchanged between the client-side visualization and the server-side business logic and data sources?* E.g., once a client modifies a certain data property, this local change has to be identified and, as a consequence, transmitted to the server-side data sources for persistence.
- *in general, how can an overall consistency between data sources and derived IVIS products be maintained?* Both sides have to be watched for occurring modification events, which trigger associated update notifications to keep data sources and information visualizations synchronized.

From the aforementioned Research Questions, the following three core functional features of the proposed IVIS infrastructure can be denoted:

- **Server Side Information Visualization:** a user (client) may request server-side application data. During the retrieval process the server transforms the requested (abstract) data into an appropriate cognitive efficient information visualization including the generation of applicable user interaction and – modification mechanisms.
- **Runtime Information Visualization:** the Runtime component comprises any user interactions in an existing visualization. In particular, users may request additional data from within the visualization or modify the displayed data content. In the latter case, any modification has to be applied to the server-side data sources as well.
- **Synchronization:** any server-side data changes must be broadcast to all affected clients to maintain consistency.

Using these three core features, the overall Research Goal can be formulated as follows. The goal is to conceptualize and develop a **generic state-of-the-art Web-based synchronization-enabled Big-Data-capable 3D IVIS infrastructure**, which may serve as a basis for various applications in different domains (concrete examples are denoted in Sect. 6). Each characterizing term of the aforementioned IVIS infrastructure implies certain requirements and further Research Challenges. The characterizing terms can be described as follows:

- **Generic:** configurable and applicable for diverse use cases
- **State-of-the-Art and Web-based:** identification and integration of contemporary (Web) technologies, approaches as well as architectural patterns serving as key system components for a modernized IVIS infrastructure.
- **Synchronization-enabled:** to permit *dynamic Raw Data* and client-side content modification on a conceptual level, the *IVIS Reference Model* should be enriched

with additional features reflecting *user-triggered update-events* and *server-side content change broadcasts*.

- **Big-Data-capable:** establish access to multiple heterogeneous data sources via the same user interface; support large datasets (challenges for processing and visualizing large datasets).
- **3D IVIS:** intuitive but powerful 3D real-time visual interface with adequate direct-manipulative IVIS interactions.

In conclusion, several research questions and challenges on the conceptual and technological levels have been recognized. With regard to the presented approach, the main challenge is how the identified core functional features can be realized on the basis of state-of-the-art technologies and key concepts like the mediator-wrapper pattern.

2.6   Research Approach

To tackle the identified Research Questions and -Objectives, the first step of our Research Approach is to perform a detailed state-of-the-art and Related Work analysis in the following areas of Computer Science: Distributed Information Systems, Information Visualization as well as contemporary Web technologies. As a result, several key concepts and system components can be identified, which will serve as a foundation to implement a prototype of the proposed IVIS infrastructure that realizes the three core functional features: *Server Side Information Visualization*, *Runtime Information Visualization* and *Synchronization*.

3   State-of-the-Art and Related Work

The discussion about contemporary technologies and approaches is presented in two subcategories. Relevant abstract concepts and architectural patterns are introduced from a scientific point of view in Sect. 3.1. Subsequently, modern technologies with regard to Web-based 3D IVIS as well as a discussion about utilizable Web protocols are addressed in Sect. 3.2. Finally, Related Work is considered in Sect. 3.3.

3.1   Scientific State-of-the-Art

Mainly, there are two relevant concepts, the *IVIS Reference Model* as the most proven visualization pipeline to transform abstract data to information visualizations [8], and the *Mediator-Wrapper* architecture, which provides a unified access to content from heterogeneous data sources [12]. Both concepts will be elaborated subsequently.

IVIS Reference Model Originally proposed by Card et al. [8], the *IVIS Reference Model* introduces three user-configurable steps to transform *Raw Data* to final *Views*, which act as a visual interface for users. The first transformation is called *Data Transformations* and filters and enriches *Raw Data* with meta-information to acquire *Data Tables* or, as a more generic term, *Structured Data*. Through *Visual Mappings*, data properties are linked to visual attributes. Finally, concrete *Views* can be generated to provide an interface for user exploration and interaction [8].

Considering current demands and challenges in the field of Big Data, Bornschlegl et al. [5] propose an extension and use the *Mediator-Wrapper* architectural pattern [29] to semantically integrate data content from multiple heterogeneous data sources, whereas the classical *IVIS Reference Model* only defined a single *Raw Data* component. Via suitable visual representations and appropriate direct-manipulative IVIS techniques, the user shall perceive core properties of huge data masses [5]. Although this extension considers Big Data challenges, it still lacks the explicit consideration of *dynamic Raw Data* (as presented in Sect. 2.2), which is a crucial requirement to synchronize data sources and information visualizations. In consequence, an additional refinement is required, as proposed in Sect. 4.1.

Mediator-Wrapper Architecture Initially proposed by Wiederhold [29], the *Mediator-Wrapper* architectural pattern defines key architectural system components to offer a homogeneous interface to access multiple heterogeneous data sources [12]. The mediation-components are embedded in a layered structure composed of the following elements, according to [12, 29]:

- **Client:** clients formulate queries against the *global schema* of the *mediator*.
- **Mediator:** the central *mediator* component manages all available data sources to mediate between them and clients. As a fundamental requirement, the mediator maintains a *global data schema*, which represents a unification of the data from all concrete data sources. Incoming queries against the *global schema* are then split up and delegated to the appropriate *wrapper* components that in turn access the actual data source.
- **Wrapper:** per data source, exactly one *wrapper* component exists that handles communication and information retrieval against a dedicated data source's *local data schema*. A crucial task of a wrapper is to reformulate an incoming query against the *global schema* into an equal query against the data source's *local schema*.
- **Data Sources:** several heterogeneous (with respect to syntax and semantic) data sources like databases or file-based formats may store relevant data. Due to syntactical and semantical differences a specific *wrapper* component per data source is required.

Concluding, the *Mediator-Wrapper* architecture may be utilized to offer a single unified interface to several heterogeneous data sources. The complexity of mediating between the *global data schema* and multiple diverse *local data schemas* is hidden from the client.

3.2 Technical State-of-the-Art

A contemporary synchronization-enabled Web-based 3D IVIS infrastructure comprises certain key technologies in the fields of appropriate 3D formats and suitable Web protocols for bidirectional communication in a client-server environment. Both aspects are discussed in the remainder of this section.

Web-based 3D Information Visualization Suitable 3D formats for Web-enabled IVIS purposes must be capable of more than mere display of virtual shapes. In particular, various event-handling mechanisms are necessary to offer powerful direct-manipulative user interactions to enhance user perception of the displayed data [9]. Promising 3D formats can, hence, be restricted to so-called *Scene Description Languages (SDL)* that organize the components of virtual shapes in tree-like hierarchies called *scene graphs* [1]. As a non-proprietary solution, the Web3D Consortium [27] recommends the ISO-certified formats *VRML* (Virtual Reality Modeling Language) and XML-based successor *X3D* (eXtensible 3D) to create arbitrary interactive virtual reality (VR) scenes.

An *X3D* browser parses the *X3D* code, which basically consists of *object-*, *sensor-*, *interpolation nodes* and so-called *ROUTE-statements*. The latter link attribute values of different *nodes* and, thus, create an event graph, which serves as a basis for animations and interactions [4]. For Web-based IVIS purposes, *X3D* browsers are available as Web browser plugins [3]. To access the *scene nodes* using a programming language, the specification defines the so-called *Scene Authoring Interface* (SAI), an Application Programing Interface (API), which is delivered with each Web browser plugin [28].

In contrast to a plugin-based integration of *X3D* into Web applications, the *X3DOM* project [2] follows a different approach. *X3D* scenes are directly embedded into the *DOM (Document Object Model)* of the Web browser and are displayed via *WebGL*. Since *WebGL* [15] is preinstalled in modern browsers, this approach overcomes the need to install an additional plugin. More importantly, each scene node of the *DOM*-embedded scene can be addressed through *JavaScript*. This simplified scene access offers a more native but equally powerful way to manipulate the scene contents without an additional API specification like the *SAI*. Moreover, the *Declarative 3D for the Web Architecture W3C Community Group* [23] identified *X3DOM* as a major candidate to embed 3D multimedia content within Web applications in a standardized manner.

In summary, client side visualization of abstract data should be done via *X3DOM*, as it presents a future-proof Web browser enabled approach for display of and interaction with 3D data.

Modern Web Protocols for Bidirectional Communication Since 2009, the WWW Consortium (W3C) specifies the *WebSocket* protocol, which establishes a full-duplex bidirectional communication channel [14]. In a client-server environment, the initial HTTP/HTTPS connection is replaced by a socket to enable each side to send arbitrary messages at arbitrary points in time. Compared to HTTP/HTTPS, the *WebSocket* protocol immensely reduces message overhead, irrelevant network traffic and complexity [24]. In particular, once established, both parties may initiate message exchange, whereas in HTTP/HTTPS only the client is able to trigger communication [24]. Developed as a key component of HTML5, the *WebSocket* protocol may act as the key technology to implement the proposed IVIS infrastructure.

3.3 Related Work

In 1999, the three functional core features (*Server Side Information Visualization*, *Runtime Information Visualization* and *Synchronization*) were realized by Leissler et al.

[18] in the course of a database-driven 3D IVIS system. As base technologies, they linked client-side *VRML* scenes, running in a Java applet, with content from a server-side relational database using an application server as middleware and the External Authoring Interface (EAI, predecessor of the SAI) to access the scene nodes from the external Java applet. To enable *VRML* scenes to interactively send queries against the database, they invented the so-called *SQL Node*, a *VRML* extension, to hold predefined SQL statements. A second *VRML* extension, the *Trigger Node*, receives trigger notifications from specified database triggers and notifies an *SQL Node* to retrieve the changed content from the database [18]. Concluding, the work of Leissler et al. represents a reference implementation with respect to our Research Goal. However, as elaborated subsequently, several improvements on a technological and conceptual level may be applied to their implementation.

3.4   Discussion and Identification of Remaining Challenges

Since the previously introduced reference implementation of Leissler et al. [18], 17 years have passed and, as identified in Sects. 3.1 and 3.2, the participating base technologies have evolved ever since. Moreover, the system of Leissler et al. is designed for a single database for content storage and access, whereas the current data landscape, specifically in Big Data scenarios, requires access to several heterogeneous data sources. In consequence, a reconceptualization and reimplementation towards a modernized and more generic IVIS infrastructure is aspirational.

For this purpose, several contemporary key technologies and abstract concepts have been identified, including:

- *X3D/X3DOM* as contemporary ISO-certified SDL to embed 3D multimedia content in Web applications,
- the *WebSocket protocol* for full-duplex bidirectional communication in a client-server environment,
- the *Mediator-Wrapper architecture* as a crucial concept to mediate between clients and multiple heterogeneous data sources in Big Data scenarios and,
- the *IVIS Reference Model* as *the* conceptual visualization pipeline to transform data content to cognitive efficient information visualizations.

Similar to Leissler et al. [18], these base technologies and concepts have to be coupled in order to obtain a generic state-of-the-art 3D IVIS infrastructure. Hence, the next step of our Research Approach demands a conceptual modeling phase.

4   Conceptual Modeling

There are two main starting points within the conceptual modeling phase. First, the concept of a synchronization-enabled visualization pipeline has to be manifested by an additional refinement of the *IVIS Reference Model*. Second, a basic abstract system architecture may serve as a foundation to find suitable coupling points between each participating key technology. Both aspects are addressed in the following subsections.

4.1 Bidirectional Extension Supporting Dynamic Data

Figure 2 presents an extension of the *IVIS Reference Model*, which explicitly allows *dynamic Raw Data* as well as data modifications.

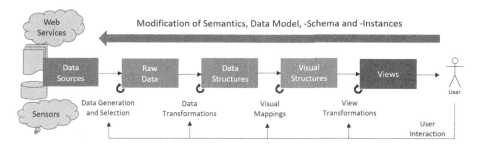

Fig. 2. Extension of the *IVIS Reference Model*

Compared to the classical *IVIS Reference Model*, the component *Data Sources* has been added to indicate that there might be multiple heterogeneous data sources, from which *Raw Data* can be acquired. The *Data Sources* component is accompanied by a new transformation called *Data Generation and Selection*, which reflects the dynamic nature of *Raw Data*. Content from *Data Sources* might be selected or dynamically generated (e.g. by simulation or computation algorithms) and the output of this transformation is then used as *Raw Data* input for the classical visualization pipeline. Notably, in the case of generated data, the *Raw Data* content is not known a priori. Another aspect is the enablement of the user to modify several aspects of the visualization pipeline, as indicated by the red backwards arrow placed at the top. Hereby, the focus of the presented research approach is to allow the modification of data instances (e.g. change properties of existing instances or create completely new instances). The presented refinement of the *IVIS Reference Model* might be utilized to match the demands of current research topics in the fields of the "Participative Web" [19] and Big Data management and visualization [5].

4.2 Conceptual System Architecture

Based on the presented key technologies, approaches and the extended *IVIS Reference Model*, Fig. 3 presents an abstract system architecture, illustrating how the key component of the proposed IVIS infrastructure work together. In particular, the composed architecture may serve as a foundation to employ the previously described extended visualization pipeline, allowing dynamic raw data as well as mediation between multiple data sources and creation of interactive visualizations.

Starting at the bottom, relevant data might be stored in several *heterogeneous data sources*. As the main component of the IVIS infrastructure, the *3DIVIS-Mediator* realizes the *Mediator-Wrapper* concept and manages communication between clients and the data source layer. This includes query handling, data source access, scene generation and delivery to the clients as well as watching for any content changes at the data tier.

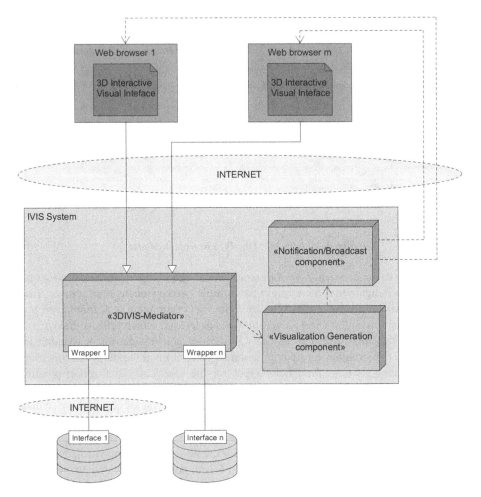

Fig. 3. Conceptual system architecture

Moreover, a *Visualization Generation* component transforms abstract data objects to concrete visualization objects, which can be delivered to clients by an additional *notification/broadcast service*. The latter may also be utilized to broadcast any content changes to all affected clients, thus, enabling the presented infrastructure to synchronize all connected clients. Eventually, on the client side, one or more users may use their Web browser to explore and perceive data through an *interactive 3D visual interface*.

Applications, built on top of this generic IVIS infrastructure, may offer cognitive efficient visual interfaces and IVIS techniques to access and analyze data from arbitrary data sources. In addition, they might offer means to persist any user-driven content modification.

5   Reference to the IVIS4BigData Reference Model

Bornschlegl et al.'s *IVIS4BigData* Reference Model [5], as introduced in Sect. 1, represents an abstract framework, where different applications and infrastructures in the fields of Big Data and Virtual Research Environments may be embedded. Within this section, it shall be analyzed, how the presented results of this paper can be integrated into the *IVIS4BigData* Reference Model.

Our Research Approach proposes a synchronization-enabled IVIS infrastructure built on the extended *visualization pipeline* from Sect. 4.1. The conceptual system architecture from Sect. 4.2 represents a specialized infrastructure capable of synchronizing heterogeneous data sources and derived 3D information visualizations. Referring to the generic IVIS infrastructure from the *IVIS4BigData* Reference Model, our approach covers several aspects and, hence, reveals multiple coupling points for integration into the work of Bornschlegl et al. [5]. For one, our approach offers access to arbitrary heterogeneous data sources by utilizing the *Mediator-Wrapper* architecture similar to Bornschlegl et al. [6]. Also our approach offers a contemporary visualization pipeline, based on a refined bidirectional *IVIS Reference Model* supporting dynamic data, to transform abstract data into cognitive efficient 3D information visualizations. Our approach, thus, might be characterized as an instance of the infrastructure of the *IVIS4BigData* Reference Model that focuses on a 3D real-time visual user interface and, in addition, provides synchronization means that enable users to persist any modification of data properties applied through the visual interface, at the associated data sources. In consequence, the *IVIS4BigData* Reference Model can be verified by our approach, which, vice versa, can also be verified, since key concepts and strategies of Bornschlegl et al.'s work [5] were applied in the conceptual system architecture.

6   Conclusion and Outlook

In conclusion, this paper identified contemporary technologies (*X3D/X3DOM*, *WebSocket* protocol) and abstract concepts (extended *IVIS Reference Model*, *Mediator-Wrapper* architecture) that can be utilized to conceptualize a generic Web-based synchronization-enabled Big-Data-capable 3D IVIS infrastructure, which integrates well into the *IVIS4BigData* Reference Model proposed by Bornschlegl et al. [5]. Ongoing research will use the extended *IVIS Reference Model* and the proposed abstract system architecture as a foundation to develop a prototypical implementation to evaluate the interplay of the participating system components. Once finished, the presented IVIS infrastructure may be utilized for various IVIS use cases. Some examples could be to visualize and analyze renewable energy generation from tidal streams [13] or provide an advanced visual interface for exploring, analyzing and annotating (to persist insight) cancer genomic data [24]. With regard to the latter, a possible benefit for an application based on the proposed IVIS infrastructure could be that several spatially distributed researches are enabled to collaboratively analyze and annotate cancer genomic data in real-time. Once researcher A persists his achieved knowledge as an annotation within the interactive visualization, it is also persisted at data source level and automatically broadcast to all other researchers visualizing the same dataset.

References

1. Bar-Zeev, A.: http://www.realityprime.com/scenegraph.php
2. Behr, J., Eschler, P., Jung, Y., Zöllner, M.: X3DOM: a DOM-based HTML5/X3D integration model. In: Proceedings of the 14th International Conference on 3D Web Technology, pp. 127–135. ACM, New York (2009)
3. Brutzman, D.: http://www.Web3d.org/x3d/content/examples/X3dResources.html
4. Brutzman, D., Daly, L.: X3D: Extensible 3D Graphics for Web Authors. Elsevier, San Francisco (2007)
5. Bornschlegl, M., Berwind, K., Kaufmann, M., Engel, F., Walsh, P., Hemmje, M., Riestra, R.: IVIS4BigData: a reference model for advanced visual interfaces supporting big data analysis in virtual research environments. In: Advanced Visual Interfaces 2016, AVI 2016, Bari (2016)
6. Bornschlegl, M., Berwind, K., Kaufmann, P., Hemmje, M.: Towards a reference model for advanced visual interfaces supporting big data analysis. In: Proceedings on the International Conference on Internet Computing, ICOMP 2016, pp. 78–81. The Steering Committee of the World Congress in Computer Science, Computer Engineering and Applied Computing (WorldComp) (2016)
7. Campesato, O., Nilson, K.: Web 2.0 Fundamentals: With AJAX, Development Tools, and Mobile Platforms. Jones & Bartlett Learning, Burlington (2010)
8. Card, S.K., Mackinlay, J.D., Shneiderman, B.: Readings in Information Visualization: Using Vision to Think. Morgan Kaufmann Publishers Inc., San Francisco (1999)
9. Chen, C.: Information Visualization and Virtual Environments. Springer Science & Business Media, Luxemburg (2013)
10. Chen, J.Q., Heath, R.D.: Web application development methodologies. In: Web Engineering: Principles and Techniques, pp. 76–96. Idea Group Inc. (IGI), Hershey (2005)
11. Dübel, S., Röhlig, M., Schumann, H., Trapp, M.: 2D and 3D presentation of spatial data: a systematic review. In: IEEE VIS International Workshop on 3DVis, pp. 11–18, IEEE Press, Paris (2014)
12. Ericsson, J.: Mediation systems: an approach to retrieve data homogeneously from multiple heterogeneous data sources. Internal report, University of Gothenburg - Department of Applied Information Technology, Gothenburg (2009)
13. Harrison, J., Uhomoibhi, J.: Engineering study of tidal stream renewable energy generation and visualization: issues of process modelling and implementation. In: AVI 2016 Workshop on Road Mapping Infrastructures for Advanced Visual Interfaces Supporting Big Data Applications in Virtual Research Environments
14. Hickson, I.: https://www.w3.org/TR/Websockets/
15. Jackson, D.: https://www.khronos.org/registry/Webgl/specs/1.0/
16. Jones, D.: http://www.teach-ict.com/as_a2_ict_new/ocr/AS_G061/311_data_info_knowledge/static_dynamic_data/miniweb/index.htm
17. Kaufmann, M.: Towards a reference model for big data management. Research report, Faculty of Mathematics and Computer Science, University of Hagen (2016)
18. Leissler, M., Hemmje, M., Neuhold, Erich, J.: Supporting image-retrieval by database driven interactive 3D information-visualization. In: Huijsmans, D.P., Smeulders, A.W.M. (eds.) VISUAL 1999. LNCS, vol. 1614, pp. 1–14. Springer, Heidelberg (1999). doi: 10.1007/3-540-48762-X_1

19. OECD: Participative Web and User-Created Content: Web 2.0, Wikis and Social Networking. OECD Publishing, Paris (2007)
20. Ortega, F., et al.: Interaction Design for 3D User Interfaces: The World of Modern Input Devices for Research, Applications, and Game Development. CRC Press, Boca Raton (2016)
21. Spence, R.: Information Visualization: An Introduction. Springer, Berlin (2014)
22. Statista. http://de.statista.com/statistik/daten/studie/13070/umfrage/entwicklung-der-internet nutzung-in-deutschland-seit-2001/
23. W3C Community Group (Declarative 3D). https://www.w3.org/community/declarative3d/
24. Walsh, P., Lawlor, B., Kelly, B., Manning, T., Heuss, T., Leopold, M.: Rapidly visualizing NGS cancer data sets with cloud computing. In: AVI 2016 Workshop on Road Mapping Infrastructures for Advanced Visual Interfaces Supporting Big Data Applications in Virtual Research Environments
25. Wang, V., Salim, F., Moskovits, P.: The Definitive Guide to HTML5 WebSocket. Apress, New York (2013)
26. Ware, C.: Information Visualization - Perception for Design. Morgan Kaufmann, San Francisco (2004)
27. Web3D Consortium a. http://www.web3d.org/x3d/why-use-x3d
28. Web3D Consortium b. http://www.Web3d.org/documents/specifications/19775-2/V3.3/Part 02/concepts.html
29. Wiederhold, G.: Mediators in the architecture of future information systems. IEEE Comput. Mag. **25**, 38–49 (1992). IEEE Press, New York

Visual Analytics and Mining over Big Data. Discussing Some Issues and Challenges, and Presenting a Few Experiences

Marco Angelini, Tiziana Catarci, Massimo Mecella[(✉)], and Giuseppe Santucci

Dipartimento di Ingegneria Informatica Automatica e Gestionale,
Sapienza Università di Roma, via Ariosto 25, 00185 Rome, Italy
{angelini,catarci,mecella,santucci}@diag.uniroma1.it

Abstract. In this short position paper, we present a few concrete experiences of Visual Analytics (VA) over big data; as our experiences have been gained on the application domains of cyber-security and Open Source Intelligence (OSINT), which are very relevant and crucial domains targets of possible Virtual Research Environments (VREs), we also discuss and propose an high-level reference architecture and pipeline for a Big Data service in VREs dealing with such aspects, in which the VA part is crucial in order to provide effectiveness to users.

1 Introduction

The availability of data has been continuously increasing over the past ten years: Web-enabled mobile devices, Web 2.0 and Internet-of-Things (IoT) technologies are among the new sources contributing to what is commonly referred to as *Big Data*. According to a *classification* proposed by *UNECE (United Nations Economic Commission for Europe)*[1], there are three main types of data sources that can be viewed as big data: *human-sourced* (e.g., blog comments), *process-mediated* (e.g., banking records), and *machine-generated* (e.g., sensor measurements).

Usable access to such complex and large amounts of data poses an immense challenge for current solutions in (visual) analytics. Handling the complexity of relevant data requires new techniques about data access, visualization, perception, and interaction for innovative and successful strategies. In addition, *Big Data services* are not easily available to all type of organizations, due to their high costs, returns on investment (ROIs) not yet clearly defined, technical challenges in setting them up, etc. Especially Small and Medium-sized Enterprises (SMEs), as well as small research teams (e.g., in small research centers and/or Universities) are faced with entry barriers. On the other side, emerging distributed, dynamic, and eventually interdisciplinary Virtual Research Environments

---

[1] cf. UNECE. Classification of types of big data. http://www1.unece.org/stat/platform/display/bigdata/Classification+of+Types+of+Big+Data. Online (accessed on 31 August 2015).

© Springer International Publishing AG 2016
M.X. Bornschlegl et al. (Eds.): AVI-BDA 2016, LNCS 10084, pp. 104–114, 2016.
DOI: 10.1007/978-3-319-50070-6_8

(VREs) can provide to scientists, industrial research users as well as to learners great opportunities for sharing such services. Already in 2010, the UK's Joint Information Systems Committee (JISC)[2] defined a VRE as a platform to help researchers from all disciplines to work collaboratively by managing the increasingly complex range of tasks involved in carrying out research on both small and large scales; they described the term VRE as "best thought of as shorthand for the tools and technologies needed by researchers to do their research, interact with other researchers and to make use of resources and technical infrastructures available both locally and nationally, [...] which also incorporates the context in which those tools and technologies are used".

In this context, our experiences that we aim at presenting to the community, are about a specific Big Data service about OSINT - Open Source INTelligence. OSINT is intelligence collected from publicly available sources ("open" refers to overt, publicly available sources, as opposed to covert or clandestine sources). This service is particularly useful in many application scenarios, such as marketing, business competitors' analysis based on social networks, emergency response, anti-terrorism activities by security agencies, etc.

In the following of this paper, we will discuss challenges of visual analytics over Big Data, and then we will present our concrete experiences in the field, based on concrete projects and activities. We also present a preliminary reference architecture for a OSINT service to be realized in VREs.

2   Visual Analytics: Issues and Challenges

As previously introduced, big data are creating unprecedented opportunities to achieve deeper, faster insights that can strengthen decision-making in different kind of environments. A key role in big data analytics is played by visualization; visualization has proven effective for not only presenting essential information in vast amounts of data but also driving complex analyses. As stated in the Intel white paper "Big Data Visualization: Turning Big Data Into Big Insights", businesses are increasingly turning to visualization-based data discovery tools, leading Gartner to estimate a 30% compound annual growth rate in the next few years. Visualization of big data helps experts visually confirm or reject hypotheses about the data and to see which data support or contradict the hypotheses; allows experts to visually find noteworthy and unusual data properties and pick interesting data samples for further analysis; allows experts to communicate a large amount of information about the data and discovered findings in an intuitive visual way and allows experts to work with the data and provide feedback about the interesting properties in data.

Visual Analytics (VA, in what follows) is a research field particularly suited for this task. Using the definition in [5], VA combines automated analysis

---

[2] cf. A. Carusi, T. Reimer. Virtual research environment collaborative landscape study. JISC, Bristol, 2010. Online: http://www.jisc.ac.uk/media/documents/publications/ vrelandscapereport.pdf.

techniques with interactive visualisations for an effective understanding, reasoning and decision making on the basis of very large and complex datasets.

At the same time, a naive application of VA principles to big data analysis could easily lead to unsatisfying results; in the following we highlight various aspects and challenges. As far as what concern this effort, different contributions can be identified that coped with the problem of applying VA to big data: among the various contributions on challenges for VA that have been proposed during the last 10 years (see [4,6–9,11]), of particular interest are the propositions in [13], that explores and classifies the state-of-the-art in terms of commercial VA tools for big data, and the work in [12] that summarizes a series of open challenges for VA directly related to extreme-scale data (petabytes and exabytes of data)

Summarizing these efforts, we can derive a focused list of open topics that should be in the agenda for research activities in the present and coming future:

1. On site analysis, where data have to be processed in memory and not transferred from disk to memory many times.
2. User interaction: the stage of interacting with visualizations is also crucial. To help domain experts analyze data, it is essential to create ways that allow them to integrate their expertise into the construction of visualizations. Interactive systems should be built to allow experts to interact with different views of data, and when those views are results of data-driven optimizations, to provide feedback about which properties of data and their relationships are most important to preserve on the visualization.
3. Novel visualization paradigms: able to abstract the data exploiting their metadata (e.g., hierarchies) and to cope with cardinality problem of big data.
4. Data reduction and dimensional reduction: the central point to cope with heterogeneous sources of big data, as clickstreams, social media, log files, streams, etc., is a way for allowing users to first represent data in a manageable form and then allowing interactive refinement of analysis, based on user needs. The stage of mapping data to visualizations is crucial and low-dimensional visualization of high-dimensional data is a challenging task. Finding informative mappings from the interesting features of data to a low-dimensional visualization is a traditional application of dimensionality reduction methods.
5. Data reduction and preservation: current best-performing dimensionality reduction methods from machine learning are non-linear mappings that are optimized to preserve essential properties of data: statistical dependencies between data features restrict data points to a manifold whose inherent dimensionality is lower than the data dimensionality. Optimizing the mappings involves modelling of important data properties and optimization of compromises necessary for presenting the properties as accurately as possible in a low-dimensional visual representation. The resulting visualizations are then integrated into the visual analytics systems for exploration of the data. Recently, methods have been proposed that improve the preservation approach even further, by connecting the preservation directly to an analysis task performed on the display.
6. Online algorithms: using incremental visualization [2] allows the user to obtain as soon as possible a visualization of the data under study, progressively

refining by itself with the addition of new data, or steerable refining accordingly to particular parameters chosen by the user in real-time (e.g., the selection of a sub-area of interest).

7. Uncertainty quantification: convey uncertainty level connected to working with data samples to the user, in order to easily communicate the degree of confidence of the visualization with respect to whole dataset.

8. Visual consistency: maintain visualization consistency, where if a big change in data occurs it is reflected proportionally in the visualization. This is an important problem tied to abstract visualization, required by big dataset cardinality, where important but sparse changes could be masked by a not consistent visual change.

3   Experiences

Having set the challenges that VA should cope with its application to big data, we present in this section important experiences we had in different domains that led us to design and development of solutions able to cope with one or more of the stated challenges. Before we want to propose a conceptual reference architecture for an OSINT service to be shared in VREs, as previously introduced, in which VA plays a relevant role.

3.1   Architectural Considerations

The main building blocks that can be identified are depicted in Fig. 1. More in details:

- **Crawling** is in charge of systematically browsing information sources (World Wide Web, social networks, forums, etc.) in order to retrieve and index contents.

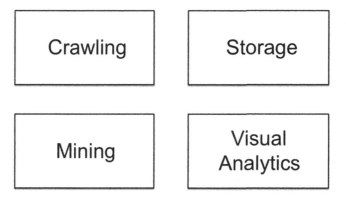

Fig. 1. Main architectural blocks

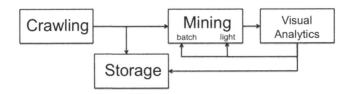

Fig. 2. Example of a possible pipeline for supporting VRE activities

- **Storage** is responsible for storing aggregated results coming from elaboration of the dataset and extracted metadata (notably in a Big Data context it is not possible to store the whole data-set).
- **Mining** allows to extract additional knowledge from the data. Given the needs for interactivity in a VRE, this can be conducted at varying levels of granularity and approximation.
- **Visual Analytics** allows the final users to easily visualize large data collections and, by interacting with it, start additional computation on the data with the final goal of making sense of the analyzed data.

Different possibilities open up by the combination of subsets of these blocks in different possible pipelines, and the creation of an efficient pipeline is in itself a field of active research. As an example, we can see a possible one in Fig. 2: the crawling is the initial block; from there data are at the same time saved for later reuse in the storage block and sent to the mining block: a combination of extracted data is then sent to the VA block; from there, the user inputs are redirected for different purposes, e.g., starting light analytics processes, or steering long batch processes with respect to user preferences, or storing subsets of the data or visualizations for later reuse or dissemination of results.

3.2   Experiences in the Cyber-Security Domain

Cyber-security is a critical domain where speed of intervention is crucial in order to identify and/or block possible threats; in this respect VA has been successfully applied in different aspects like log analysis, network protection, etc. The raising dimension of networks and the vast amount of sensors that collect various information about devices and network nodes makes the problem of cyber-defending a network a big data problem. Main experiences here have been conducted in the form of designing and developing beyond state-of-the-art solutions for the PANOPTESEC project[3]. The PANOPTESEC project aims at delivering a beyond-state-of-the-art prototype of an automated cyber defence decision support system to demonstrate operational use of dynamic risk approaches for automated cyber defence algorithms, architecture and design. In this context, a VA solution has been designed and developed to provide to a security operator the maximum degree of situational awareness in order to support time-constrained decision making.

---

[3] EU FP-7 Panoptesec project, http://www.panoptesec.eu.

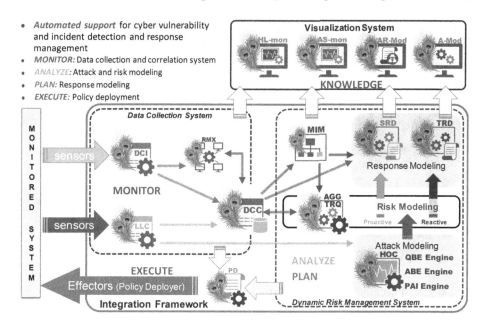

- *Automated support* for cyber vulnerability and incident detection and response management
- *MONITOR:* Data collection and correlation system
- *ANALYZE:* Attack and risk modeling
- *PLAN:* Response modeling
- *EXECUTE:* Policy deployment

Fig. 3. The PANOPTESEC system architecture: on top the Visual Analytics Environment layered in its high level tasks is visible, connected both ways with the rich back-end in charge of computing and analyzing big cyber-security data

The PANOPTESEC system (see Fig. 3), and in particular the Visual Analytics Environment, is structured in a serie of high level task visualizations (Analysis & Maintenance, Monitoring, Attack Response, High level management) that gather data from a rich common back-end and then present them with different visual paradigms to different users (security administrators, system administrators, security operators, managers). In this way different users can inspect, reason and interact with Big Data produced by the back-end, putting in the field their different expertise but contributing altogether to the extraction of additional knowledge used again in the loop for steering back-end computation.

In order to cope with sheer amount of data (tens of thousands of nodes, each producing hundred of thousands of log entries per second) designed solutions exploited inner hierarchies in the data and abstract visualizations in order to reduce and aggregate data presented to the user, still allowing her to refine the analysis. We developed various proposals on network visualizations (see [3] and Fig. 4), vulnerability assessment and monitoring (see Fig. 5), and reaction to possible attack scenarios (see [1]). While in the *Monitoring task* the solution in Fig. 4 can help a security operator and also an environmental researcher to manage and analyze the possible consequences that a cyber-attack on SCADA systems can have on the territory, the solution in Fig. 5, deployed in the *Analysis and Maintenance task*, can help in analyzing the vulnerability state of the network nodes in order to prevent possible attacks and strengthen the defense of the

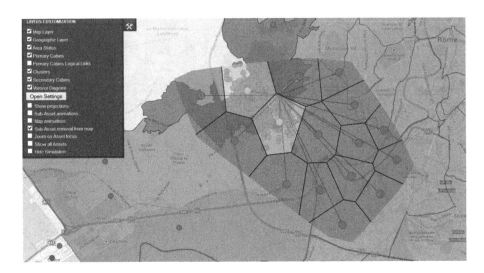

Fig. 4. Visual geographical representation of a 13.000 nodes network with hierarchical aggregation on both domain and geographical layers. Single nodes are color coded from full green to full red based on their risk levels. Risk level of a geographical area results from the aggregation of single risk levels using various functions (e.g., max, average) with the same color scale. Finally a Voronoi map is used to cluster hierarchically lower levels node into one single entity. (Color figure online)

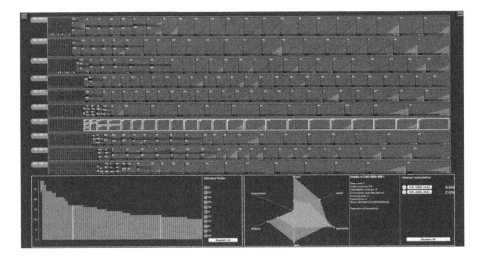

Fig. 5. Visual abstract representation of the same network, focusing on vulnerabilities and business mission impact. Each rectangle represents a network node, with its area mapping the number of vulnerabilities, and the area and color of the inner triangle representing the average criticality and mission impact respectively. On the lower left part is possible to explore a frequency distribution of the vulnerabilities on a sub-selection of nodes, while on the lower right part is possible to inspect characteristics of selected vulnerabilities using a radar chart.

critical infrastructures. Notably, in these experiences they have been investigated solutions for points 2, 3 and 4 as discussed in Sect. 2.

3.3 Experiences in the Web Intelligence Domain

The main issues with OSINT raise from the needs to process lot of information from heterogeneous sources (social networks, forums, etc.) with tight time-constraints. In our initial experimental projects, we are adopting an approach based on a pool of Web/social crawlers, which collects data and inject them into a distributed messaging system based on Apache Kafka, to be finally sent to different pipelines of analysis, managed through Apache Spark. Results of the computations are stored in a distributed file system (HBASE) and then sent to the upper layers, in which is located the Visualization and Visual Analytics environment. This architecture, visible in Fig. 6, has proven to be general enough in order to insert several types of analysis, ranging from data mining algorithms to Natural Language Processing (NLP) ones.

Also in this scenario is strong the need for having an environment that allows multiple actors to conduct their analysis: with regards to them, and with consideration regarding the 4 V's of Big Data, is clear that not all of them can be computed in real-time or on-demand. In this case the solutions for VA applications can adopt the following approach: one part of the computation can produce results after a fixed time interval (depending on the amount of data and the specific algorithms; we refer to it as batch computation); an example with respect to the shown architecture can be a serie of Spark processes computing time consuming algorithms on the data. The user will interact with the results, indexed in fast-response environment (e.g., Elastic Search) with a subset of faster algorithms in order to quickly refine the analysis, allowing fast interaction and manipulation of the data in order to obtain additional information: this gathered information will be used both as an outcome for propagation to other tasks of

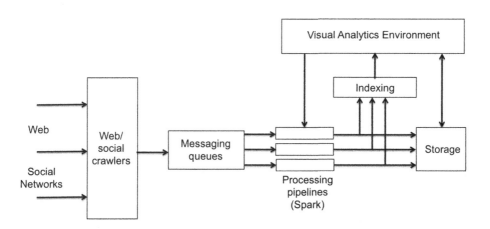

Fig. 6. High-level architecture for a Visual Analytics system for OSINT

analysis and as an additional input to steer the batch computation in the next time interval, with the final goal of optimizing the quality of the results of the batch computation with respect to the user's task. Notably, in these experiences they have been investigated solutions for points 1, 2 and 5 as discussed in Sect. 2.

3.4   Incremental Visualization

Our research effort also focus on providing a methodology to cope with high cardinality and dimensionality of the dataset in incremental way. We need to provide incremental computation, from both the data and the process point of view; the former means chunking data in a smart way and applying algorithms on a chunk at a time, while the latter means producing approximated results, using low computational version of an algorithms, and step-by-step refining these results. According to Shneiderman [10], VA is useless if the system does not allows for quick interaction (e.g., 10 frames per second updates) while exploring data. This approach has the big advantage of allowing the user a quick interaction with initial partial results, and the possibility, where previously designed, to steer the computation towards particular interesting areas of the dataset that are coming out from the user comprehension of initial results. In the context of Big Data this can constitutes an edge in allowing fast reasoning and hypotheses formulation, yet on partial representation of the data. Two contributions ha been proposed, one applicative in the form of an application for car incident datasets (see [2]) and one presenting a methodology and formal model for designing inherently incremental Visual Analytics applications (see Fig. 7)

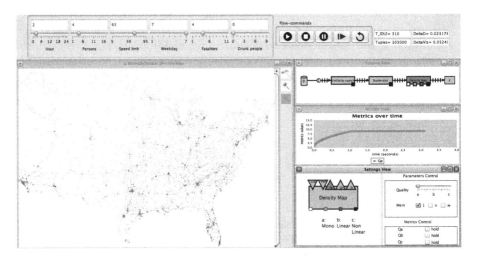

Fig. 7. Example of an application designed using the proposed model and framework: on the left is visible the actual visualization of incrementally refined results; on top-right is visible the model of the incremental application; on bottom right the designer can parametrize single blocks in terms of quality or quantity of each incremental output; finally, on middle-right the designer can inspect quality metrics in order to find a better parametrization

In these experiences they have been investigated solutions for points 2, 5 and 6 as previously discussed.

4   Concluding Remarks

In this short position paper, we have presented a few concrete experiences gained on real projects dealing with Visual Analytics over big data, discussing how they represent (partial) solutions to challenges identified in the literature. Clearly more research is needed on these topics. At the same time, our experiences have been gained on the application domains of cyber-security and OSINT, which are very relevant and crucial domains targets of possible VREs. We have therefore also proposed an high-level reference architecture and pipeline for a Big Data service in VREs dealing with such aspects, in which the VA part is crucial in order to provide effectiveness to users.

We would like to conclude this paper by discussing how the research here presented can be contextualized wrt. the IVIS4BigData reference model [14], cf. Fig. 8.

In particular, our work can be associated to the *Data collection, management and curation* module, as crawling for OSINT is a specific acquisition technique for open sources. As far as the *Knowledge-based support* and the *User empowerment*, our approach is based on the continuous interplay between incremental visualization and batch analytical tasks, especially in the case of interactive analyses. In our case, *Analytics* is heavily based on the Apache toolbox, in particular on the Spark programming model.

With high similarity to this reference model, also the PANOPTESEC system (see Fig. 3), and in particular the Visual Analytics Environment, is structured in a serie of high level task visualizations that gather data from a rich common back-end and then present them with different visual paradigms to different users.

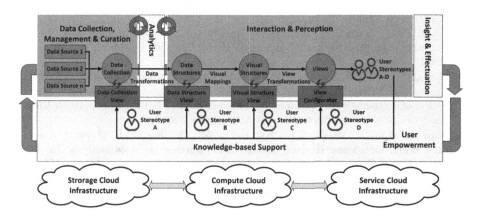

Fig. 8. IVIS4BigData reference model

Acknowledgments. This work has been partly supported by the EU FP7 project PANOPTESEC, and the Italian projects Social Museum e Smart Tourism (CTN01_00034_23154), NEPTIS (PON03PE_00214_3), and RoMA - Resilence of Metropolitan Areas (SCN_00064).

References

1. Angelini, M., Prigent, N., Santucci, G.: Percival: proactive and reactive attack and response assessment for cyber incidents using visual analytics. In: 2015 IEEE Symposium on Visualization for Cyber Security (VizSec), pp. 1–8. IEEE (2015)
2. Angelini, M., Santucci, G.: Modeling incremental visualizations. In: Proceedings of the EuroVis Workshop on Visual Analytics (EuroVA 2013), pp. 13–17 (2013)
3. Angelini, M., Santucci, G.: Visual cyber situational awareness for critical infrastructures. In: Proceedings of the 8th International Symposium on Visual Information Communication and Interaction (2015)
4. Jagadish, H., Gehrke, J., Labrinidis, A., Papakonstantinou, Y., Patel, J.M., Ramakrishnan, R., Shahabi, C.: Big data and its technical challenges. Commun. ACM **57**(7), 86–94 (2014)
5. Keim, D.A., Kohlhammer, J., Ellis, G., Mansmann, F.: Mastering the information age-solving problems with visual analytics (2010)
6. Keim, D.A., Kohlhammer, J., Santucci, G., Mansmann, F., Wanner, F., Schaefer, M.: Visual analytics challenges. In: eChallenges 2009 (2009)
7. Keim, D.A., Mansmann, F., Schneidewind, J., Ziegler, H.: Challenges in visual data analysis. In: Information Visualization (IV 2006). IEEE (2006)
8. Keim, D.A., Mansmann, F., Schneidewind, J., Thomas, J., Ziegler, H.: Visual analytics: scope and challenges. In: Simoff, S.J., Böhlen, M.H., Mazeika, A. (eds.) visual data mining. LNCS, vol. 4404, pp. 76–90. Springer, Heidelberg (2008). doi:10.1007/978-3-540-71080-6_6
9. Sedig, K., Ola, O.: The challenge of big data in public health: an opportunity for visual analytics. Online J. Public Health Inform. **5**(3), 223 (2014)
10. Shneiderman, B.: Extreme visualization: squeezing a billion records into a million pixels. In: SIGMOD 2008 (2008)
11. Thomas, J., Kielman, J.: Challenges for visual analytics. In: Information Visualization 2009 (2009)
12. Wong, P.C., Shen, H.-W., Johnson, C.R., Chen, C., Ross, R.B.: The top 10 challenges in extreme-scale visual analytics. IEEE Comput. Graph. Appl. **32**(4), 63 (2012)
13. Zhang, L., Stoffel, A., Behrisch, M., Mittelstadt, S., Schreck, T., Pompl, R., Weber, S., Last, H., Keim, D.: Visual analytics for the big data era - A comparative review of state-of-the-art commercial systems. In:2012 IEEE Conference on Visual Analytics Science and Technology (VAST). IEEE (2012)
14. Bornschlegl, M.X., Berwind, K., Kaufmann, M., Hemmje, M.L.: Towards a reference model for advanced visual interfaces supporting big data analysis. In: 17th International Conference on Internet Computing and Internet of Things, ICOMP 2016 (2016)

A Meta-design Approach to Support Information Access and Manipulation in Virtual Research Environments

Carmelo Ardito[1], Maria Francesca Costabile[1], Giuseppe Desolda[1(✉)],
Maristella Matera[2], and Paolo Buono[1]

[1] Dipartimento di Informatica, Università degli Studi di Bari Aldo Moro,
Via Orabona, 4, 70125 Bari, Italy
{carmelo.ardito,mariafrancesca.costabile,giuseppe.desolda,
paolo.buono}@uniba.it
[2] Dipartimento di Elettronica, Informazione e Bioingegneria, Politecnico di Milano,
Piazza Leonardo da Vinci, 32, 20134 Milan, Italy
maristella.matera@polimi.it

Abstract. Virtual Research Environments (VREs) are distributed and dynamic software environments that foster the collaboration of people from different disciplines by supporting the accomplishment of complex research tasks. VREs lack efficient and effective user interfaces able to satisfy the needs of the different types of people collaborating in performing certain tasks. Thus, a great challenge that VREs have to address is user diversity, which arises from different factors such as cultural background of users, their reasoning strategies, the way they carry out their tasks in their daily practices, and the languages and notations they are familiar with. This paper provides a solution to this challenge by proposing to create VREs that exploit the meta-design approach we have developed to design interactive systems that address user diversity. We then describe a mashup platform, built according to the meta-design approach, which supports non-technical users in accessing and manipulating information in VREs by enabling them to extract contents from heterogeneous sources and manipulate such content in their personal interactive environments, thus creating new content that can be shared among people collaborating to a task in a VRE. Finally, it is briefly discussed how this platform can be useful in some phases of the recently proposed model of Information Visualization for Big Data.

Keywords: Mashups · Web composition environments · Data integration · Data visualization

1   Introduction

The huge amount of data available today (so-called Big Data) requires "new techniques about data access, visualization, perception, and interaction for supporting innovative and successful information strategies" [1]. Up to now, such data are primarily managed and used by computer scientists. The opportunity offered by today's technology can enable people with different expertise, operating on different application domains and

M.X. Bornschlegl et al. (Eds.): AVI-BDA 2016, LNCS 10084, pp. 115–126, 2016.
DOI: 10.1007/978-3-319-50070-6_9

not necessarily expert of computer science (non-technical users), to directly access and work with a same portion of data. Thus, the concept of VRE (Virtual Research Environments) can be enforced through the creation of distributed, dynamic and interdisciplinary software environments that can provide the possibility to exploit such data to academic scientists, industrial research users, as well as learners in computer science and/or data science. VREs should allow people from diverse disciplines "to work collaboratively by managing the increasingly complex tasks involved in carrying out research on both small and large scales. However, these VREs lack cognitive-efficient and effective Human-Computer Interaction (HCI) support and overall interoperability in existing approaches" [1].

Because of the great variety of people collaborating through VREs, one main requirement of efficient and effective VRE interfaces is to address user diversity. This has been a concern of our research for many years. Indeed, based on our wide experience in observing people working with interactive systems, we are well aware that even people working in a same application domain and using the same system are often diverse, constituting different (sub-)communities characterized by specific cultures, goals, tasks and context of activity [2, 3]. To offer a proper user interface, it is of critical importance to address this user diversity [4]. This is a big challenge for VREs. The slogan "one size fits all" does not work: different users of a same interactive system may need different interfaces able to provide them with adequate support. In other words, people need user interfaces that should be designed by taking into account their cultural background, their reasoning strategies, the way they carry out their tasks in their daily practices, the languages and notations they are familiar with.

This paper provides a solution to the challenge of addressing user diversity by proposing to create VREs by means of a *meta-design* methodology. According to this approach, an interactive system should propose different interaction environments, each one suited to a specific community of users, adopting a language for the human-computer dialog inspired by languages and notations used in the community's daily practice [2]. The approach aims also to accommodate the increasing need of users for tailoring the systems they use. People are willing to perform various activities that involve modification or even creation of software artifacts. Such activities range from simple parameter customization to more complex activities, like variation and assembling of components [5, 6]; they are examples of End-User Development (EUD) activities, as defined in [7]. In short, end users are becoming co-designers of their software tools and services [8]. Consequently, professional designers (software engineers) have to create software environments that can empower end users to shape the software they use, without obliging them to become programmers.

This paper discusses all the previous aspects to show how meta-design can help design VREs that can be easily adapted to the needs of different users communities. After summarizing the meta-design paradigm, in Sects. 2 and 3 describes how the EFESTO mashup platform exploit this approach to enable non-technical users with varying skills and background to access and manipulate information in VREs; the scenario presented in Sect. 4 shows how end users extract content from heterogeneous sources available online, manipulate and integrate such content in personal interactive environments to create new content that can be shared among people collaborating to a certain task in a VRE. Being "road mapping infrastructures for advanced information visualization supporting big data application" the main topic of this book, Sect. 5 discusses how EFESTO can be useful in some phases of the recently proposed model of Information Visualization for Big Data called *IVIS4BigData* [1]. Section 6 briefly reports related work about mashups. Finally, Sect. 7 provides the conclusion.

2 Meta-design of Interactive Systems

In order to build systems that allow end users to create and modify software artifacts, a two-phase design process must be considered, which requires a shift in traditional design paradigms, moving from participatory design to meta-design, which literally means "design for designers" [2, 8]. In the first phase of this process (meta-design phase), designers and expert programmers design and develop the design environments, i.e., the environments suited to the diverse stakeholders who participate in the design of the final applications. In the second phase, the end-users exploit the ready-to-use design environments and the tools available in such environments, in order to design their final applications. The two phases are not clearly distinct, and may be executed several times in an interleaved way because the design environments evolve as a consequence of both the progressive insights the different stakeholders gain into the design process and the feedbacks provided by end users working with the system in the field.

Over the years, we have been working on the creation of software infrastructures for different domains, to support EUD activities as well as knowledge creation and sharing among the involved stakeholders. This research resulted in the definition of a design approach based on the Software Shaping Workshop (SSW) model, which allows a team of experts to cooperate in the design, development, use and evolution of interactive systems [2, 9–11]. Instead of developing the final interactive system, as it happens in traditional design approaches, the SSW model guides professional developers in designing software environments (meta-design phase) that will be then used by different stakeholders, not only to carry out specific tasks at use time, but also to contribute to the design and evolution of the interactive system (design phase, performed by end users at use time) [3]. These software environments are called Software Shaping Workshops (SSWs or briefly workshops). The term workshop comes from the analogy with an artisan's workshop (e.g., the joiner's or the smith's workshop), i.e., the workroom where the artisan finds all and only those tools necessary to carry out her/his activities. Each SSW provides an interaction language tailored to its users' culture, since it is defined by formalizing the traditional user notations and system of signs [12]. Communication channels among the various workshops are provided in order to support collaborative development and evolution of both system and tasks. Thus, the workshops act as cultural mediators among the different stakeholders by presenting the shared knowledge according to their own languages [11]. The SSWs are designed according to the "gentle slope of complexity" principle [4, 6, 13]: people find in their SSW only those tools and functionalities necessary to their tasks, presented in a way that is adequate to their culture and skills, so that they can easily use them. Of course, once users get familiar with their

SSW, they may require new and more complex functionalities: such needs likely crop up later on, determined by users' evolution during time.

The SSW methodology has been applied in several projects, as reported in [3].

3   Empowering End Users to Compose Heterogeneous Resources

VREs need effective access, management and usage of resources during "collaborative research processes, where intermediate results have to be shared between interdisciplinary teams and their organizations in scientific communities or industry" [1]. The EFESTO (EFesto End uSer composition plaTfOrm) mashup platform [14] successfully responds to this need, as it will be shown in Sect. 4. The name recalls Efesto, a god of the Greek mythology who realized magnificent magic arms for other Greek gods and heroes. Analogously, the EFESTO platform aims to put in the hands of end users powerful tools to let them accomplish their tasks. The development of the platform was carried out in accordance with the meta-design model, which is instrumental to permit the customization of the platform to specific application domains and communities of users, in order to be actually usable for its users.

Different stakeholders are involved in the overall design. The first meta-design phase consists of designing software environments that allow some stakeholders to create templates, basic elements, and software environments appropriate for end users in the specific application domain; in the second phase, using the environments devoted to them, end users are able to compose and manipulate the resources of interest.

The traditional two-phase meta-design model has been extended in order to address the activities performed to customize the platform to specific domains of interest. The result is a three-layer model briefly described here. At each layer, either activities of meta-design, or a mix of design and use activities are performed, depending on the different stakeholders involved. Indeed, professional developers perform meta-design, since they create the software environments (SSWs) for all the other stakeholders involved in the design and implement and/or modify the software artifacts that require programming efforts (top layer in Fig. 1). In order to facilitate the composition process by end users the composition environments (bottom layer in Fig. 1) needs to be customized to their needs.

The middle layer in Fig. 1 refers to another meta-design phase, during which professional developers and domain experts work together to customize the general-purpose tools by selecting and packaging service-based components that are adequate for specific scenarios in a certain application domain, and also by implementing specific visual templates and tools, that end users can fruitfully exploit to create their Interactive Workspaces (IWs). Services registered in the platform, visual templates and tools are resources made available in the end users' IWs. The tools embed the logic, defined by the domain experts, for allowing end users to easily querying services, integrating the retrieved results and properly visualizing them. End users' IWs are deployed on different devices, e.g., a PC, a tablet, a multi-touch large device (bottom layer in Fig. 1).

The collaboration of professional developers and domain experts is essential for a successful customization. In fact, domain experts are familiar with the types of

Meta design by
professional developers

Integrated development environments (IDEs) for:
* Implementing software environments for other stakeholders
* Implementing visual templates

Meta-design for customization
by Domain experts
in collaboration with
Professional developers

Platform environment for:
* Service selection
* Service registration
* Service composition
* Visual template selection
* Tool selection

Design by
End users
at use time

Mashup tool for:
* Workspace creation
* Workspace use
* Workspace edit

Fig. 1. Meta-design approach to the creation of interactive environments for different stakeholders. The top layer refers to the meta-design activities of professional developers, who program the basic elements (service descriptors and visual templates) later used by the other stakeholders. The middle layer refers to the customization activities. The bottom layer shows the Interactive Workspace for end users, deployed on different devices [15].

information end user would retrieve, the manipulations they would perform and the most suitable visualizations. However, they do not know how to access the services on the Web that can provide specific information. On the other hand, professional developers are able to set up the service access and also create proper visualizations by using Web technologies (for example HTML and JavaScript) or specific languages for other devices (e.g., Java for Android).

4   Use of a Mashup Platform in a VRE: A Scenario

According to our meta-design model, different tools can be developed during the customization phase so that they can foster data visualization and manipulation by different people. In the following, a scenario illustrates how VREs can take advantage of our model and platform.

The scenario shows how different stakeholders of a big company are supported in retrieving, composing, analysing and manipulating data. Different types of people work collaboratively by managing big data and increasingly complex tasks, in order to carry out their work. Let us suppose that an American big company specialized in electronics is going to develop a new OLED display. Managers, designers, engineers, sales experts, and staff are involved in this complex task. In order to take decisions about design, development, and marketing strategy, the company first analyses and manages competitors, market products, as well as its internal resources. The mashup platform supports all the stakeholders by providing proper data sources and tools to let them getting the data of interest and organizing them as they wish.

Before releasing the platform inside the company, it was customized according to the company needs. In particular, a set of data sources and tools of interest were identified, so that they will be easily used by the different stakeholders. Since the company certainly wants to be informed about competitors and their products, some of the identified sources refer to companies that sell similar products, or to the products themselves, to market statistics, etc. In addition, to foster easier data visualization and manipulation by each stakeholder, different tools were developed, for example: a *Forecasting* tool that can be useful for managers and sales experts to predict market statistics; a *Comparing* tool for designers and managers to make comparisons, e.g., of competitor products; a *Locating* tool for the geo-localization of entities, e.g. the company competitors.

At use time, each stakeholder uses the mashup platform by adding data sources of interests into his (let us suppose the user is a male) IW, organizing the retrieved data according to his needs by means of specific visualizations (e.g. *list*, *map*, and *graph*) available in the platform, and also manipulating such data through operations such as union and join, which are performed through simple visual mechanics, since the platform addresses non-technical users, who do not know terms like union and join [14, 16]. The created workspaces can be saved and shared with other stakeholders. Collaboration is also supported on shared workspaces [17, 18].

It is worth remarking another very innovative feature of the EFESTO platform: the tools it offers implement functionality that enable specific tasks: such tools allow users to manipulate the information in a novel fashion, i.e., without being constrained to pre-defined operation flows typical of pre-packaged applications. With reference to our scenario, company employees can exploit the available tools to perform more specific and complex sense-making tasks. For example, if a sale expert has to decide where to sell the new OLED display, he could be interested in looking where the company competitors are located. Thus, he retrieves the list of competitors from the *Companies* data source, which are then shown in a window (Fig. 2, circle 1), and then drags the desired competitors inside the *Locating* window where a map is displayed (Fig. 2, circle 4). In this way, the companies are visualized as pins on the map. The *Locating* window was previously opened by clicking on the *Locating* tool in the menu on the left. Similarly, if designers want to compare the features of some competitors' products, they use the *Products* data source (Fig. 2, circle 2) and the *Comparing* tool, moving some products inside the *Comparing* window once it is opened (Fig. 2, circle 3).

The previous examples show that the flow of the operations performed by users is not pre-defined a priori but is determined at runtime, by the users themselves, according to their exploration needs/desires arising during the interaction. This flexibility is a significant feature of EFESTO; it implements some of the Transformative User experience principles described in [19, 20]. Alternatively, the sale expert could first look at a specific product and find out where they are primarily sold. In this case, he retrieves a list of products from the Product data source, which are shown in a window and then drugs some of them in the Comparing window to compare their technical features. Then,

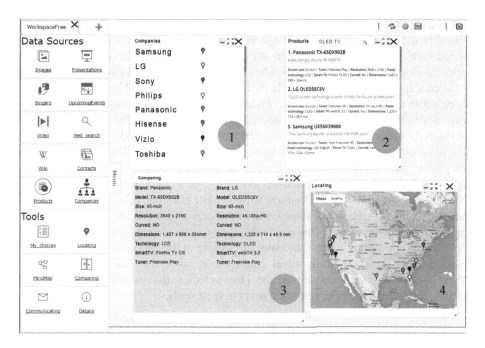

Fig. 2. Workspace created with two data sources (Companies and Products) and two tools (Comparing and Locating).

he selects a couple of them that he finds interesting and drags them in the Locating window to visualize where such products are sold.

Field studies were performed in specific application domains in order to validate the first version of the EFESTO platform [15, 17, 21]. Such studies highlighted new users' requirements, which currently are not satisfied by any mashup tool. Among the most important ones, there is the need to perform join operations with data sources that can fulfil the various users' desires of detailed information. Indeed, despite their growing availability, APIs typically describe a portion of a domain and often do not include many details able to satisfy complex users information needs. In order to overcome this drawback, the novelty of the EFESTO platform is to allow end users to exploit the big data collection made available by the Linked Open Data (LOD) by means of a *polymorphic data source* (PDS). The term "polymorphic" indicates the possibility for the user to select the data attributes that are more pertinent with respect to the mashup under construction. In other words, the user can self-define every time a new API on top of LOD that exploit the big quantity of data to satisfy their situational needs.

For more details the reader may refer to [22, 23].

Let us briefly describe the value of the PDS by going back to our scenario. The *Products* data source (Fig. 2, circle 2) does not provide technical specification about the display technology (it only specifies the type, for example LED, OLED, etc.). Since this information is not available in an API, the user can exploit the PDS data source available in EFESTO in order to extend the *Products* data source with the details he wants. To do this, the user clicks on the gearwheel icon at the top-right corner of the *Products* data source and then clicks on the "Extend data source with details" menu item to activate a wizard procedure that assists in this operation (which is technically a join). When the wizard starts, the user first indicates the attribute he wants more details about (*technology* in this case), and then selects the PDS. The platform shows a list of PDS attributes related to the concept of *technology* available in the DBpedia ontology. The user then creates the new data source, which extends the *Products* data source, with *description* and *patent* attributes, which are the details he is interested in. Henceforward, the user accessing the *Products* data source finds a list of competitor products on the market, of which he can also get additional information about the *technology* attribute. The user could keep composing the *Products* data source with the PDS by starting from other *Products* attributes. For each attribute he decides to extend, the PDS provides further attributes related to the semantics of the *Products* attribute. For example, by extending the *Brand* attribute of the *Products* data source, PDS attributes like *headquarter* and *number of employees* would be shown. This is why this type of data source is said *polymorphic*: it provides different information (attributes) according to the data source attribute that is selected. This is a significant novel contribution, since the standard data sources (YouTube, Wikipedia, etc.) provide the same set of attributes independently of the selected attribute, thus greatly limiting users in their wishes.

5   Visual Analysis of Big Data: The Mashup Platform May Help

The IVIS4BigData model shown in Fig. 3 has been recently introduced in [1]. It revises the Information Visualization reference model presented in [24], in order to make it suitable to Big Data Management. The first phase, *Data Collection, Management and Curation*, includes all the procedures to access, compose and visualize data sources. Starting from the data produced in this phase, the *Analytics* phase introduces tools to transform and process data by means of statistical methods also exploiting specific visualization (e.g. correlation graph). The third phase, *Interaction & Perception*, consists of tools to visualize data and interact with them. The last phase is the *Insight & Effectuation* and consists of a set of decision-making tools to help experts in situations of uncertainty. In all these phases, different stakeholders are involved.

With respect to this IVIS4BigData model, our mashup platform supports users operating on different application domains to directly access and work with a same portion of data. For example, as described in the scenario reported in the previous section, company employees can access to the same data sources, compose them by exploiting join and union operations performed through visual mechanisms and use different User Interface (UI) templates to get different perspectives on the same data. In particular, the scenario described the creation of a workspace in which the users added the *Companies* and *Products* data sources, the last one also extended by using the PDS. These features provided by EFESTO cover the *Data Collection, Management & Curation* phase of the IVIS4BigData model.

In the scenario, the EFESTO tools were also presented as important components to provide task-related functions for manipulation and transformation of data along user-defined task flows. In particular, two tools were used, *Locating* and *Comparing*, which

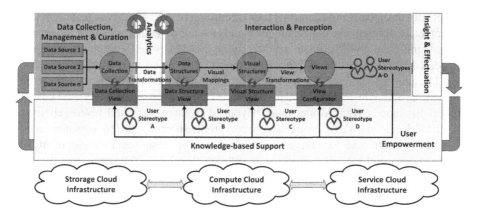

Fig. 3. A process of a Virtual Research Environment presented in [1].

represent a typical example of activities carried out in the *Interaction & Perception* phase of the IVIS4BigData model. A more powerful tool, *Forecasting*, provides analytics functions to support sales manager. Tools for analytics operations (like *Forecasting*) are useful in the *Analytics* phase of the IVIS4BigData model.

6   Related Work About Mashups

This paper illustrated how the EFESTO mashup platform can support information access and manipulation of VREs. This section therefore briefly reports related work about mashups to let the reader understand how EFESTO is positioned and which are its characterizing features with respect to other similar works. Our approach indeed especially addresses the definition of VREs through the integration of data and functionality offered by Web APIs and data sources.

Several mashup methods and tools have been proposed in the last two decades, characterized by different composition paradigms in order to facilitate mashup by non-technical users. One of the pioneers (even if it is not available anymore) was *Yahoo! Pipes* [25] that, in the attempt to better support end users, provided a visual editor to access services and operators visualized as visual modules that could be combined into a canvas pane by means of 'pipes' through drag and drop actions. In the successive years, several mashup tools based their composition approaches on the Yahoo!Pipes paradigm. However, despite the wire paradigm was claimed to be very promising for not-technical users, it did not succeeded because some factors limited the adoption of these mashup tools in real contexts. Indeed, some user-centric studies found that their composition paradigms are still difficult to master for non-technical users because the adopted composition languages do not fit their mental model [26–28]. This problem pushed researchers in investigating mashup tools implementing different paradigms. An example was *NaturalMash,* a tool that allows users to express in natural language what service(s) they need to use and how to synchronize them [29]. Another approach was proposed in PEUDOM, a platform that exploits drag&drop mechanisms to aggregate widgets in a dashboard and connected them according to an event-driven paradigm [18]. A completely different mashup technique avoids the use of remote resources and enables data integration allowing users to act directly on the Web page UI elements, which are considered interactive artifacts that can be combined through a set of mashup operations [30]. Despite this approach appears very promising, some limitations still affect this solution, for example, low performance (UIs need to be instantiated locally), the missing support for more advanced use cases beyond data integration and heterogeneity of structured data in the Web. A book that is a comprehensive reference for mashups covers the main concepts and techniques underlying mashup design and development, the synergies among the models involved at different levels of abstraction, and the way models materialize into composition paradigms and architectures of corresponding development tools [31]. Other mashup tools and mashup techniques are described in [31, 32].

EFESTO represents an important contribution to the state of the art since it introduces different features that aim to satisfy the end users needs and foster its adoption in real contexts. We just mention two of such features. First, it implements an interaction paradigm that, as shown in the field studies [15, 17, 21], enables users without skills in computer programming to extract content from heterogeneous services and integrate them into newly created applications accessible through different devices [16]. Second, it exploits the Linked Open Data cloud to create an enormous data source called *Polymorphic Data Source* [22, 23], which allows users to get detailed information satisfying their diverse needs.

7 Conclusion

In this paper, we discussed the meta-design model we have defined to design interactive systems. In particular, the model has been adopted to create a mashup platform, called EFESTO, which enables non-technical users to access and manipulate heterogeneous resources available on Internet. We have shown that this platform supports different types of people in accessing and manipulating information during collaborative tasks carried out in VREs.

User diversity is addressed by customizing the interactive environments with respect to the needs and characteristics of the users they are devoted to. In this way, the general-purpose platform can be adapted every time a new application domain has to be addressed, to provide end users with the capability to self-organize and customize their final applications and data.

The customization to a new domain is usually performed once. Further customization might occur, in order to satisfy specific needs emerging later, e.g., to register or to combine further services.

Innovative features of EFESTO have been briefly presented. First, the availability of the polymorphic data source defined on the Linked Open Data, which allows end users to get more detailed information they may need and that API(s) are not able to provide. Second, the flexibility of the user interface, i.e., the possibility end users have to perform operations without being constrained by a pre-defined operation flow, but instead deciding at runtime what they want to do, in order to satisfy their exploration desires arising during the interaction.

The paper concludes by discussing the use of the EFESTO platform during some phases of the Information Visualization for Big Data model proposed in [1]. The EFESTO platform has been validated in various contexts in which different people perform collaborative tasks [15, 17, 21]. Specific studies addressing the management of Big Data are part of future work.

References

1. Bornschlegl, M.X., Berwind, K., Kaufmann, M., Engel, F.C., Walsh, P., Hemmje, M.L.: IVIS4BigData: a reference model for advanced visual interfaces supporting big data analysis in virtual research environments. In: Proceedings of IVIS4BigData: A Reference Model for Advanced Visual Interfaces Supporting Big Data Analysis in Virtual Research Environments (2016)
2. Costabile, M.F., Fogli, D., Mussio, P., Piccinno, A.: Visual interactive systems for end-user development: a model-based design methodology. IEEE Trans. Syst. Man Cybern. Part A Syst. Hum. **37**(6), 1029–1046 (2007)
3. Ardito, C., Buono, P., Costabile, M.F., Lanzilotti, R., Piccinno, A.: End users as co-designers of their own tools and products. J. Vis. Lang. Comput. **23**(2), 78–90 (2012)
4. MacLean, A., Carter, K., Lövstrand, L., Moran, T.: User-tailorable systems: pressing the issues with buttons. In: Proceedings of CHI 1990, Seattle, pp. 175–182 (1990)
5. Mørch, A.I., Stevens, G., Won, M., Klann, M., Dittrich, Y., Wulf, V.: Component-based technologies for end-user development. Commun. ACM **47**(9), 59–62 (2004)
6. Wulf, V., Pipek, V., Won, M.: Component-based tailorability: enabling highly flexible software applications. Int. J. Hum Comput Stud. **66**(1), 1–22 (2008)
7. Lieberman, H., Paternò, F., Wulf, V. (eds.): End User Development. Springer, Netherlands (2006)
8. Fischer, G., Giaccardi, E., Ye, Y., Sutcliffe, A.G., Mehandjiev, N.: Meta-design: a manifesto for end-user development. Commun. ACM **47**(9), 33–37 (2004)
9. Costabile, M.F., Fogli, D., Fresta, G., Mussio, P., Piccinno, A.: Building environments for end-user development and tailoring. In: Proceedings of HCC 2003, 28–31 October 2003, pp. 31–38 (2003)
10. Costabile, M.F., Fogli, D., Mussio, P., Piccinno, A.: End-user development: the software shaping workshop approach. In: Lieberman, H., Paternò, F., Wulf, V. (eds.) Is-EUD 2006, vol. 9, pp. 183–205. Springer, Netherlands (2006)
11. Cabitza, F., Fogli, D., Piccinno, A.: Fostering participation and co-evolution in sentient multimedia systems. J. Vis. Lang. Comput. **25**(6), 684–694 (2014)
12. Iverson, K.E.: Notation as a tool of thought. Commun. ACM **23**(8), 444–465 (1980)
13. Spahn, M., Dörner, C., Wulf, V.:. End user development: approaches towards a flexible software design. In: Proceedings of ECIS. Galway, pp. 303–314 (2008)
14. Desolda, G., Ardito, C., Matera, M.: EFESTO: a platform for the end-user development of interactive workspaces for data exploration. In: Daniel, F., Pautasso, C. (eds.) RMC 2015. CCIS, vol. 591, pp. 63–81. Springer, Heidelberg (2016). doi:10.1007/978-3-319-28727-0_5
15. Ardito, C., Costabile, M.F., Desolda, G., Lanzilotti, R., Matera, M., Piccinno, A., Picozzi, M.: User-driven visual composition of service-based interactive spaces. J. Vis. Lang. Comput. **25**(4), 278–296 (2014)

16. Ardito, C., Costabile, M.F., Desolda, G., Lanzilotti, R., Matera, M., Picozzi, M.: Visual composition of data sources by end-users. In: Proceedings of AVI 2014. Como, 28–30 May, pp. 257–260 (2014)

17. Ardito, C., Bottoni, P., Costabile, M.F., Desolda, G., Matera, M., Picozzi, M.: Creation and use of service-based distributed interactive workspaces. J. Vis. Lang. Comput. **25**(6), 717–726 (2014)

18. Matera, M., Picozzi, M., Pini, M., Tonazzo, M.: PEUDOM: a mashup platform for the end user development of common information spaces. In: Daniel, F., Dolog, P., Li, Q. (eds.) ICWE 2013. LNCS, vol. 7977, pp. 494–497. Springer, Heidelberg (2013). doi: 10.1007/978-3-642-39200-9_43

19. Latzina, M., Beringer, J.: Transformative user experience: beyond packaged design. Interactions **19**(2), 30–33 (2012)

20. Beringer, J., Latzina, M.: Elastic workplace design. In: Wulf, V., Schmidt, K., Randall, D. (eds.) Designing Socially Embedded Technologies in the Real-World, pp. 19–33. Springer, London (2015)

21. Ardito, C., Costabile, M.F., Desolda, G., Latzina, M., Matera, M.: Hands-on Actionable Mashups. In: Díaz, P., Pipek, V., Ardito, C., Jensen, C., Aedo, I., Boden, A. (eds.) IS-EUD 2015. LNCS, vol. 9083, pp. 295–298. Springer, Heidelberg (2015). doi: 10.1007/978-3-319-18425-8_33

22. Desolda, G.: Enhancing workspace composition by exploiting linked open data as a polymorphic data source. In: Damiani, E., Howlett, R.J., Jain, Lakhmi, C., Gallo, L., De Pietro, G. (eds.). SIST, vol. 40, pp. 97–108Springer, Heidelberg (2015). doi: 10.1007/978-3-319-19830-9_9

23. Desolda, G., Costabile, M.F.: Building data sources with linked open data to enrich mashup platforms. In: Proceedings of SEBD 2016, Ugento, 19–22 June 2016

24. Card, S.K., Mackinlay, J.D., Shneiderman, B.: Readings in Information Visualization: Using Vision to Think. Morgan Kaufmann Publishers Inc., San Francisco (1999)

25. Pruett, M.: Yahoo!Pipes. O'Reilly, Sebastopol (2007)

26. Namoun, A., Nestler, T., Angeli, A.: Conceptual and usability issues in the composable web of software services. In: Daniel, F., Facca, F.M. (eds.) ICWE 2010. LNCS, vol. 6385, pp. 396–407. Springer, Heidelberg (2010). doi:10.1007/978-3-642-16985-4_35

27. Casati, F.: How end-user development will save composition technologies from their continuing failures. In: Costabile, M.F., Dittrich, Y., Fischer, G., Piccinno, A. (eds.) IS-EUD 2011. LNCS, vol. 6654, pp. 4–6. Springer, Heidelberg (2011). doi: 10.1007/978-3-642-21530-8_2

28. Namoun, A., Wajid, U., Mehandjiev, N.: Service composition for everyone: a study of risks and benefits. In: Dan, A., Gittler, F., Toumani, F. (eds.) ICSOC/ServiceWave -2009. LNCS, vol. 6275, pp. 550–559. Springer, Heidelberg (2010). doi:10.1007/978-3-642-16132-2_52

29. Aghaee, S., Pautasso, C.: End-user development of mashups with NaturalMash. J. Vis. Lang. Comput. **25**(4), 414–432 (2014)

30. Daniel, F.: Live, personal data integration through UI-oriented computing. In: Cimiano, P., Frasincar, F., Houben, G.-J., Schwabe, D. (eds.) ICWE 2015. LNCS, vol. 9114, pp. 479–497. Springer, Heidelberg (2015). doi:10.1007/978-3-319-19890-3_31

31. Daniel, F., Matera, M.: Mashups: Concepts, Models and Architectures. Springer, Heidelberg (2014)

32. Lemos, A.L., Daniel, F., Benatallah, B.: Web service composition: a survey of techniques and tools. ACM Comput. Surv. **48**(3), 1–41 (2015)

IVIS4BigData: Qualitative Evaluation of an Information Visualization Reference Model Supporting Big Data Analysis in Virtual Research Environments

Marco Xaver Bornschlegl[(✉)]

Faculty of Mathematics and Computer Science,
University of Hagen, 58097 Hagen, Germany
`marco-xaver.bornschlegl@fernuni-hagen.de`

Abstract. Handling the complexity of relevant data (generated through information deluge and being targeted with Big Data technologies) requires new techniques with regard to data access, visualization, perception, and interaction for innovative and successful strategies. As a response to increased graphics performance in computing technologies and information visualization, Card et al. developed the Information Visualization Reference Model. Due to further developments in Information Systems as well as Data Analysis and Knowledge Management Systems in recent years, this reference model has to be adapted for addressing the recent advancements. Thus, the hybridly refined and extended IVIS4BigData Reference Model was derived from the original model to cover the new conditions of the present situation with advanced visual interfaces providing opportunities for perceiving, managing, and interpreting Big Data analysis results to support insight and emerging knowledge generation.

After deriving the IVIS4BigData Model, the necessity to evaluate the appropriateness of this reference model existed. In this context, a full day workshop on Road Mapping Infrastructures for Advanced Visual Interfaces Supporting Big Data Applications in Virtual Research Environments was proposed and conducted at the Advanced Visual Interfaces conference 2016. This focused event for virtual research environment and human computer interaction research experts was utilized to present, discuss, and evaluate the derived IVIS4BigData reference model. In order to validate some of the properties of the derived model in a kind of pre-testing evaluation, all of these experts were asked to take part in a questionnaire before the start of the workshop and the corresponding results are outlined within this paper.

Keywords: IVIS4BigData · Advanced visual user interfaces · Distributed big data analysis · Information visualization · User empowerment · Virtual research environments

© Springer International Publishing AG 2016
M.X. Bornschlegl et al. (Eds.): AVI-BDA 2016, LNCS 10084, pp. 127–142, 2016.
DOI: 10.1007/978-3-319-50070-6_10

1 Introduction and Motivation

Handling the volume and complexity of relevant data in Virtual Research Environments (generated through information deluge and being targeted with Big Data technologies) requires new techniques with regard to data access, preparation, analysis, visualization, perception, and interaction for supporting emerging knowledge generation, informed decision making and corresponding successful research, innovation, and business development strategies. As a consequence virtually collaborating interdisciplinary research communities as well as industrial research organizations, but especially research teams at small universities and **Small and Medium-sized Enterprises (SMEs)**, will be faced with enormous challenges. Furthermore, current e-Science research resources and infrastructures (i.e., data, tools, and related **Information and Communication Technology (ICT)** services) are often confined to computer science expert usage only and fail to leverage the abundant opportunities that distributed, dynamic, and eventually interdisciplinary **Virtual Research Environments (VREs)** can provide to scientists, industrial research users as well as to learners in computer science, data science and related educational environments.

As a response to increased graphics performance in computing technologies and information visualization, Card et al. [7] developed the **Information Visualization (IVIS)** Reference Model, that is illustrated in Fig. 1.

Due to further developments in Information Systems as well Data Analysis and Knowledge Management Systems in recent years, this reference model has to be adapted for covering the recent advancements. Therefore, Bornschlegl et al. proposed the **Road Mapping Infrastructures for Advanced Visual Interfaces Supporting Big Data Applications in Virtual Research Environments** workshop [5] at the **Advanced Visual Interfaces (AVI)** conference 2016 [6] where academic and industrial researchers and practitioners working in the area of Big Data, Visual Analytics, and Information Visualization were invited to discuss future visions of Advanced Visual Interface infrastructures supporting Big Data applications in Virtual Research Environments. Within that context, the **IVIS4BigData** Reference Model was presented and qualitatively evaluated in a road mapping activity.

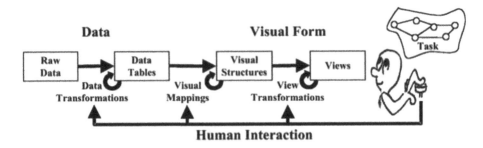

Fig. 1. Information visualization reference model [7]

2   IVIS4BigData Reference Model

As illustrated in Fig. 2, Big Data Analysis supporting emerging knowledge generation and innovation-oriented decision making is based on different perspectives and intentions. To support management functions in their ability of making sustainable decisions, Big Data Analysis specialists are filling the gap between Big Data Analysis result consumers and Big Data technologies. Thus, *"these specialists need to understand their consumers/customers intentions as well as a strong technology watch, but are not equal to developers, because they care about having impact on the business"* [23].

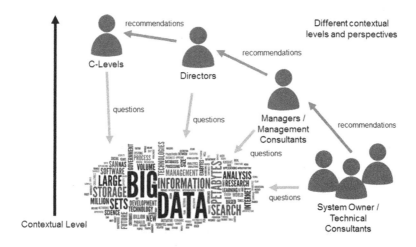

Fig. 2. Big Data perspectives in industry [3]

Deduced from these perspectives and intentions, there are different use cases and related user stereotypes that can be identified for performing Big Data analysis collaboratively within an organization seeking to support emerging knowledge generation and innovation. Users with the highest organizational knowledge and competence levels like, e.g., managers of different hierarchy levels of such organizations, need to interact with visual analysis results for their decision making processes. On the other hand, users with low organizational knowledge and competence levels, like system owners or administrators, need to interact directly with data sources, data streams or data tables for operating, customizing or manipulating their systems and contents. Nevertheless, user stereotypes with lower organizational knowledge and competence levels are interested in visualization techniques as well, in case these techniques are focusing on their lower organizational knowledge and competence levels. Finally, there are user stereotype perspectives in the middle of those levels, representing the connection between user stereotypes with low and high contextual knowledge and competence levels. Business Analysts or Business Intelligence Consultants in consultancy scenarios are filling the gap between Big Data consumers and Big Data technologies and often interact with both, low level data streams and visualization technologies. As a consequence from these various perspectives and contextual organizational knowledge and competence levels, it is important to provide the different user stereotypes with a kind of context aware information technology infrastructure to support their individual use cases. *"The 'right' information, at the 'right' time, in the 'right' place, in the 'right' way to the 'right' person"* [12]. One could add to this citation *"with the right competences"* or *"with the right user empowerment"*.

Modern cloud technologies and distributed computing technologies are leading to almost unlimited storage and computing performance. Moreover, usable access to complex and large amounts of data over several data sources requires new techniques for accessing and visualizing data with innovative and successful strategies, at the border between automated data analysis, research insight, and business innovation decision making [13]. Being not in full alignment with these new required techniques, the original IVIS Reference Model only supports transforming data from a single data source on the left directly to a visual representation for the end user on the right, without a direct view and interaction possibility in the single process stages.

Thus, the hybridly refined and extended IVIS4BigData Reference Model [4] (cf. Fig. 3), an adaptation and extension of the original IVIS Reference Model, in combination with Kaufmann's Big **Data Management (BDM)** Reference Model [16] was achieved to cover the new conditions of the present situation with advanced visual interface opportunities for perceiving, managing, and interpreting Big Data analysis results to support insight, emerging knowledge generation and informed decision making. In this way, the derived model became integrated with the underlying reference model for BDM which illustrates different stages of BDM. This means, the adaptation of the IVIS Reference Model represents the interactive part of the underlying BDM life cycle.

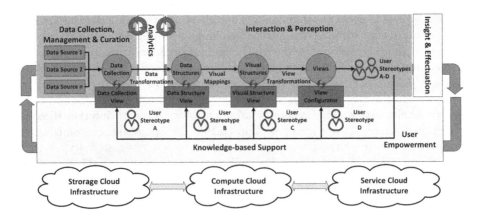

Fig. 3. IVIS4BigData reference model [4]

According to Card et al., functions which indicate a series of (multiple) data transformations lead from raw data to data presentation for humans. However, instead of collecting raw data from a single data source, multiple interdisciplinary cross-domain and cross-organizational data sources have nowadays to be connected, integrated by means of appropriate information integration approaches like mediator wrapper architectures, and in this way globally managed in **Data Collections** inside the **Data Collection, Management & Curation** layer. Therefore, the first consecutive transformation which is located in the **Analytics** layer of the underlying BDM model, maps the data from the connected data sources into **Data Structures** which represent the first stage in the **Interaction & Perception** layer. The generic term **Data Structures** also includes the use of modern **Big Data Storage Technologies** (like, e.g., NoSQL, RDBMS, HDFS), instead of using only data tables with relational schemata. In the following step **Visual Mappings** which transform data tables into **Visual Structures** and **View Transformations** which create **Views** of the **Visual Structures** by specifying graphical parameters such as position, scaling, and clipping, do not differ from the original IVIS reference model. As a consequence, only interacting with analysis results does not lead to any *"added value"* for the optimization of, e.g., research results or business objectives. Furthermore, no process steps are currently located within the **Insight & Effectuation** layer because such *"added value"* is rather generated from knowledge, which is a *"function of a particular perspective"* [18] and will be generated within this layer by combining the analysis results with existing knowledge.

Therefore, the major adaptations are located between the cross-functional **Knowledge-Based Support** layer and the corresponding layers above. As a consequence from the various perspectives and contextual levels of Big Data analysis and management user stereotypes, additional visual interaction features lead from the human users on the right into multiple visually-interactive user interface **Views**. These functional arrows are illustrating the visually direct manipulative interaction between user stereotypes with single process stages and the adjustments of the respective transformations by user-operated user interface controls to provide *"the 'right' information, at the 'right' time, in the 'right' place, in the 'right' way to the 'right' person"* [12] within a context aware and user-empowering system for individual use cases. Finally, the circular iteration around the whole set of layers clarifies that IVIS4BigData is not aiming at supporting solely an one time process because the results can be used as the input for a new process iteration.

3   User Study

After deriving the IVIS4BigData reference model which covers the new conditions of the present situation with identifying advanced visual user interface opportunities for perceiving, managing, and interpreting distributed Big Data analysis results, the necessity to evaluate the reference model still existed. Moreover, potential use case scenarios, user stereotypes, and their required competencies for applying the presented model with focus on supporting management functions, as key consumers of Big Data Analysis in Virtual Research Collaboration and Business Innovation and Intelligence scenarios, needed to be examined.

In this context, a full day workshop on **Road Mapping Infrastructures for Advanced Visual Interfaces Supporting Big Data Applications in Virtual Research Environments** [5] at the **Advanced Visual Interfaces (AVI)** conference 2016 [6], was utilized to present, discuss, and evaluate the derived IVIS4BigData Reference Model. In this way, the communities of the AVI conference which are consisting of academic and industrial researchers and practitioners, working in the area of Big Data, Visual Analytics, and Information Visualization was invited to discuss future visions of Advanced Visual Interface infrastructures supporting Big Data applications in Virtual Research Environments.

3.1   Method

Instead of a public meeting, this workshop was organized as a focus event (expert roundtable) for invited researchers (domain experts) of accepted research papers after a public call for participation where all submissions were reviewed by an international expert programme committee. Therefore, the results gathered by using the round table methodology are very significant for evaluating the IVIS4BigData Reference Model, even with only eight representative expert participants being present at the workshop. This evaluation strategy of expert roundtables with experts from relevant domains is a long established evaluation technique [21,25], and thus highly acknowledged in research. It arose out of a need for consensus-building to identify problems, explore solutions, and define actions in the relationship between formal decision makers such as judiciaries and governments and other sectors of society during the 1980's [9,20].

After a short introductory presentation, each expert participant representing one of the eight accepted workshop papers and therefore one of the corresponding research domains related their Big Data research in their Virtual Research Environment domains ([1,2,8,10,14,19,22,24]) presented their research domain paper within a 20 min time frame. Following the presentations of the participants, the organizers presented their derived IVIS4BigData Reference Model which had also been used as the reference framework for the road mapping development of the workshop. For defining their relationships to the derived model and at the same time for starting to validate the derived IVIS4BigData Reference Model, all of the representatives were asked to take part in a kind of pre-testing questionnaire[1] until the start of the workshop. This questionnaire was separated in 10 categories with 49 questions in total (General Information (4), Academic Background (3), Research Area (4), Big Data Application Domain/Data Science Domain (6), Data Characteristics (4), Data Interaction (5), Big Data Technologies (11), Big Data Visualization (6), End User Empowerment (4), and Software Framework (2)), and consisted of both free-text and multiple-choice questions.

---

[1] http://goo.gl/forms/0dlKNdWNsvQS3qQv1.

3.2   Results

Demographics. The experts (responding representatives of the eight accepted workshop papers and corresponding research domains) came from six different research institutions in five different countries (United Kingdom (3), Italy (2), Germany (1), Republic of Ireland (1), and Switzerland (1)). Seven of these experts came from the university sector and one came from the industrial sector. In total, 34 researchers of 13 different research institutions in 6 different countries (Germany (12), Italy (10), United Kingdom (6), Republic of Ireland (4), Switzerland (1), and Spain (1)) were involved in the 8 accepted papers. 28 of the total participants came from the university sector and 8 from the industrial sector.

Related to the academic degree, 50% of the experts hold a Ph.D. degree (or equivalent), 37.5% hold a Full Professor's degree, and 12.5% hold a Bachelor's degree (or equivalent). The experts were specialized in a wide field of study within the field of Computer Science. Seven different fields of study can be identified based on their indications to the relating free-text question (Human Computer Interaction (3 respondents), Computer Science (2), Bio Informatics (1), Data Management (1), Geo Informatics (1), Medical Informatics (1), and Web Engineering (1)). The average number of publications is 85.4, whereas 25% of the experts have contributed to 0–10 publications, 25% of the experts have contributed to 11–50 publications, 12.5% of the experts have contributed to 51–100 publications, and 37.5% of the experts have contributed to more than 100 publications.

The size of the research groups of the experts is distributed among three values (1–5 researchers (37.5%), 6–10 researchers (25%), and more than 10 researchers (37.5%)). 100% of the research groups contain PHDs, 87.5% of the research groups contain Ph.D. Students, 37.5% of the research groups contain Students (graduated), and 25% of the research groups contain Students (not graduated). Results show that, in addition to the wide field of study, the group of respondents is characterized by high educational background and in depth research experience.

End User Stereotypes and Human Computer Interaction. The experts were asked about Human Computer Interaction of different end user stereotypes in the process phases of their research project's advanced Big Data application with regard to the phases of the IVIS Reference Model. End user stereotypes were clustered in four different groups relating to our assumption in Fig. 2 which has been already presented as well as initially discussed and validated during an earlier expert round table at the EGI[2] Community Forum Conference 2015 [15]. In the context of that conference, the end user stereotypes were focusing on Big Data applications from a management perspective. To be more generic and to include consultancy scenarios as well, we generalized the labels of the four different end user stereotypes as follows; System Owner - System Owners/Technical

---

[2] European Grid Initiative.

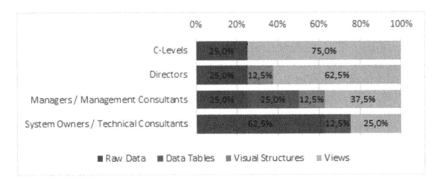

Fig. 4. Interaction between user stereotypes and IVIS reference model phases

Consultants, Department Manager - Managers/Management Consultants, Area Manager - Directors, Managing Directors - C-Levels. Figure 4 illustrates the results of the Human Computer Interaction of different end user stereotypes in the process phases of the IVIS Reference Model.

With this illustration, observations that support the relation between the user stereotypes outlined in Fig. 2 and the derived model can be made. This figure indicates, e.g., a relationship between the contextual knowledge and competence levels of the end user stereotypes and the data abstraction level. Whereas System Owners with a lower contextual level are only interacting 25% with user interface views, this value increases continuously up to 75% for C-Levels with the highest contextual organizational knowledge and competence level. Therefore, the observations also support our assumption that users with the highest contextual organizational knowledge and competence level, like e.g. managers of different hierarchy levels of organizations, need to interact with visual analysis results for their decision making processes. On the other hand, users with low contextual organizational knowledge and competence levels, like system owners or administrators, need to interact directly with data sources, data streams or data tables for operating, customizing or manipulating their systems.

Moreover, also the assumption that Business Analysts or Business Intelligence Consultants in consultancy scenarios often interact with both, low level data streams and visualization technologies, is supported by the observations of the interaction results. In addition to their interaction with Raw Data and Views, those user stereotypes, that can be assigned to the level System Owner up to Director in reference to their Big Data consume, are interacting with Data Tables and Visual Structures as well.

Nevertheless, the result also indicates that Raw Data must be rated high. Although System Owners are representing the most important end user group, in relation to the Raw Data phase with an interacting rate of 62.5%, 25% of all other end user stereotypes with higher contextual organizational knowledge and competence levels are interacting with this phase of the IVIS Reference Model, too.

Data Science Competencies. Only an organizations' technical ability for Big Data analysis does not automatically result in a corresponding availability of appropriate human resources. In addition to the questions about the end user stereotypes above and to derive the end users competencies, the participants were asked several questions about the Big Data Application Domain/Data Science Domain of their Advanced Big Data Application.

The first question addressed the application domain of the research outcome. Seven different application domains can be identified based on their indications to the relating free-text question (Data Mining (50% of the Advanced Big Data Applications), Business Intelligence (25%), Human Computer Interaction (25%), Web Engineering (12.5%), Information Visualization (12.5%), Healthcare (12.5%), and Knowledge Management (12.5%)).

In the second question of this category the participants were asked for the educational levels of user stereotypes, that will apply the Advanced Visual Big Data Application. The results of this multiple choice question yield that 87.5% of the Advanced Big Data Applications are addressing users with academic background, and only 12.5% are addressing users without academic background. Another 62.5% are addressing users with management background, and only 25% are addressing users with technical background. Only applications that are addressing users with academical background are addressing users with technical and management background as well.

"Big Data analysis specialists are filling the gap between Big Data analysis result consumers and Big Data technologies" [3]. Thus, *"these specialists need to understand their consumers/customers intentions as well as a strong technology watch, but are not equal to developers, because they care about having impact on the business"* [23]. To derive the competencies of Big Data analysis specialists (*"the new profession Data Scientist"* [17]) for designing, establishing, operating and customizing Big Data analysis infrastructures as well as extracting

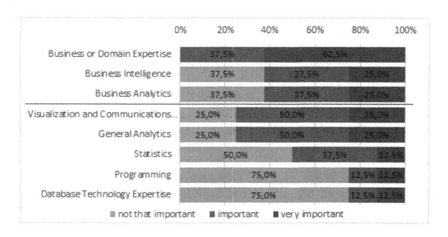

Fig. 5. End user competencies to apply advanced Big Data applications

meaningful value from the Big Data analysis results, the participants were asked for the competencies, that are required to apply their Advanced Visual Big Data Application. Figure 5 illustrates the results of this question.

In this illustration, the competencies were clustered in two different groups. In the lower rungs are technical competencies ordered from Database Technology Expertise until Visualization and Communication Expertise. The upper rungs from Business Analytics to Business or Domain Expertise represent the business specific competencies. The representation indicates a trend between the disposal and the importance of the different competencies. It can be observed, that the business specific competencies of the upper rungs are classified as more important than the technical competencies within the lower rungs. Thus, considering all of the values within the cluster, the business specific competencies were rated by 37.5% as very important, by 37.5% as important, and by 25.0% as not that important on average. Whereas the technical competencies are only rated by 17.5% as very important, by 32.5% as important, but by 50% as not that important on average.

Moreover, it can also be observed, that the importance of the competencies increases with their level. Whereas only 12.5% of the participants rate Database and Technology expertise as important, this rate increases up to 25% with regard to Visualization and Communication Expertise and further on up to 62.5% with regard to Business or Domain Expertise.

The observations of the results in this category support our assumption that *"Data Scientists need a technical understanding of Big Data as well as a professional understanding of their customers contextual levels and perspectives"* [3]. Moreover, our assumption that there are different use cases and related user stereotypes that can be identified for performing Big Data analysis collaboratively within an organization can also be supported by the results.

Information Visualization. The major adaptation between the IVIS Reference Model and the derived IVIS4BigData reference model are multiple user interface views, that allow the interaction of the end user with single process stages and the adjustments of the respective transformations by user-operated controls. To evaluate the need of our assumption, the participants were asked which phases of the IVIS Reference Model their Advanced Big Data Application tries to visualize. Figures 6 and 7 are illustrating the results to this question.

As expected by means of the results of the interaction between different user stereotypes and the IVIS Reference Model phases, that relate closely to this question, a visualization need of each phase can be clearly identified. The Raw Data phase was visualized in 50%, the Data Table phase in 37.5%, the Visual Structures phase in 62.5%, and the Views phase in 100% within the advanced Big Data application of the respondents. In addition to these values, Fig. 7 shows a more detailed result of the visualized phases in the respondents' Big Data applications.

In this figure, a similarity between the different Advanced Big Data Applications of the respondents can be observed. 37.5% (3, 4, and 7) of the respondents

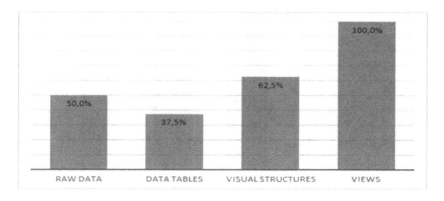

Fig. 6. Visualization of IVIS reference model phases - overview

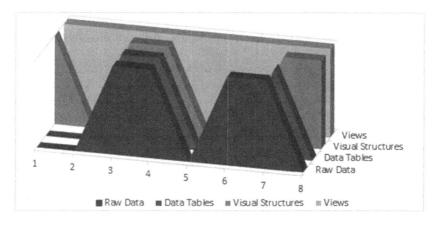

Fig. 7. Visualization of IVIS reference model phases - detailed

are visualizing all phases of the IVIS Reference Model, 25% (2) are visualizing only Views, 25% (1 and 8) are visualizing Visual Structures and Views, and 12.5% (6) are visualizing Raw Data and Views. These results support the adaptation of the IVIS Reference Model with the additional Views on each phase and the corresponding arrows from the human user stereotypes on the right into the Views.

IVIS4BigData Architecture. Integrated into the underlying reference model for BDM, which illustrates different stages of BDM, the adaptation of the IVIS Reference Model represents the interactive part of the BDM life cycle. For evaluating the assignment of the original IVIS phases into the BDM layers within the IVIS4BigData Reference Model, the participants were asked before the presentation of IVIS4BigData how they would assign the layers of the BDM Reference

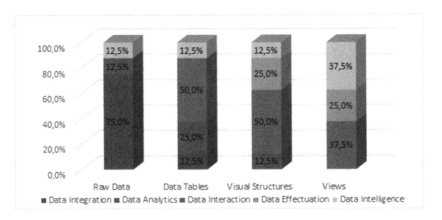

Fig. 8. Assignment of BDM layers to IVIS phases

Model to the phases of the IVIS Reference Model. Figure 8 illustrates the result
to this question.

In this illustration, with the exception of the Views phase (37,5% Data Interaction as well as 37,5% Data Intelligence assignment), all IVIS phases lean
towards a special layer of the BDM Reference Model (Data Integration with
an assignment rate of 75% to Raw Data, Data Interaction with an assignment
rate of 50% to Data Tables, and Data Interaction also with an assignment rate
of 50% to Visual Structures). Despite the balanced assignment rate of the Views
phase, an observation that supports our assignment of IVIS phases to BDM
layers can be made from this result. In correspondence with our hypothesized
assignment, the participants of the expert round table assigned the IVIS phases
to the same BDM layers as our IVIS4BigData model. This interpretation can be
based on the fact that each IVIS phase has its maximum assignment rate to the
BDM layer IVIS4BigData placed it.

Moreover, it can also be observed that the assignment of the Data Interaction
Layer is remarkable high relating to the Data Table, Visual Structure, and Views
phases. This observation supports the assumption that most of the IVIS phases
are allocated within the Data Interaction layer. Another remarkable observation
is related to the assignment values of the Data Intelligence layer. Although the
assignment rates are small, it is the only BDM layer that is assigned to each IVIS
phase. This result supports the assumption that the Data Intelligence Layer can
be seen as a cross functional layer where all of the IVIS phases can be accessed.

IVIS4BigData Integration. In addition to the initial assessment questionnaire, the workshop participants elaborated during the remainder of the workshop on how their research application could be assigned to and supported by
the derived IVIS4BigData Reference Model. Main outcome of this expert round
table discussion within the workshop was, that each party mentioned that their
respective virtual research work infrastructure can be assigned to specific parts

of the introduced model. Indeed the different research groups are often using only individual and non-integrated parts of the IVIS4BigData reference model, all of them agreed that this model can represent a framework for their representing Virtual Research Environment's IT infrastructure as well as a generic framework for supporting distributed Big Data analysis applications to support emerging knowledge generation in interdisciplinary research collaboration as well as in cross-domain and cross-organizational Business Intelligence and corresponding innovation scenario.

Limitations. The small number of participants in this study could be a limitation of this work, due to a limited significance of the user study. The group of participants in this survey was characterized by high educational backgrounds and in depth research experience within their corresponding fields of study. Although the participants of the workshop were well chosen through a review process by an international programme committee, the results of this study have a restricted generalizability in regard to people with other educational backgrounds or research experiences in other fields of study.

3.3   Conclusion

The results of the user study are justifying the demand for the adaptation of the IVIS Reference Model. Indeed the different research groups are often using only individual and non-integrated parts of IVIS4BigData, all of them agreed that this model can represent a framework for their research as well as a generic framework for distributed Big Data analysis applications to support Business Intelligence. The participants of the expert round table assigned the IVIS phases to the same BDM layers as our IVIS4BigData model suggests. Moreover, the demand for the major adaptation of the IVIS Reference Model - the additional Views for a visualization possibility in each phase and the corresponding arrows from the human user stereotypes on the right to the Views - can be validated. Additionally, the hypothesized interaction between different user stereotypes and the IVIS Reference Model phases were also proved by the results of our study.

Within this study, also different use cases and end user stereotypes for performing Big Data analysis collaboratively within an organization can be identified. Furthermore, with focus on the Data Science competencies the results are highlighting, that the importance of the competencies increases with their level. This supports the initial assumption that *"Data Scientists need a technical understanding of Big Data as well as a professional understanding of their customers contextual levels and perspectives"* [3]. Summarizing all results of the study, it can be concluded that IVIS4BigData satisfies the demands of the new situation provided by advanced visual interface opportunities for perceiving, managing, and interpreting Big Data analysis results.

4   Discussion and Outlook

This paper presents a user study that evaluates the demand of the IVIS4BigData Reference Model, as well as potential use case scenarios, user stereotypes, and their required competencies for applying the presented model with focus on supporting management functions, as key consumers of Big Data Analysis in Business Intelligence scenarios. Summarizing all results of the study, it can be concluded that IVIS4BigData satisfies the demands of the new situation provided by advanced visual interface opportunities for perceiving, managing, and interpreting Big Data Analysis results. Moreover, as the main outcome of the expert round table discussion within the workshop, each party mentioned that their respective work can be situated in specific parts of the introduced model.

The study supports the assumption that users with the highest contextual organizational knowledge and competence level, like e.g. managers of different hierarchy levels of organizations, need to interact with visual analysis results for their decision making processes. On the other hand, users with lower contextual levels, like system owners or administrators, need to interact directly with data sources, data streams or data tables for operating, customizing or manipulating their systems. Nevertheless, the result also shows that Raw Data must be rated high. Although System Owners are representing the most important end user group in relation to the Raw Data phase, all other end user stereotypes with higher contextual levels are interacting with this phase of the IVIS Reference Model, too. Therefore, this phase has to be elaborated in more detail in further research activities.

Indeed the different research groups are often using only individual and non-integrated parts of IVIS4BigData, all of them agreed that this model can represent a framework for their research as well as a generic framework for distributed Big Data analysis applications to support Business Intelligence, which will be a further challenge within this research. For achieving an usable and sustainable implementation of the developed reference model in practice, the design of a conceptual *Service-Oriented Architecture (SOA)*, that must ensure easy operability as well as a certain flexibility for special accommodations by their customers, is planned. After designing the architecture, the integration of certain presented Advanced Big Data Applications of the workshop as bookable service modules within this framework is intended.

 Acknowledgments and Disclaimer. This publication has been produced in the context of the EDISON[3] project [11]. The project has received funding from the European Union's Horizon 2020 research and innovation programme under grant agreement No 675419. However, this paper reflects only the author's view and the European Commission is not responsible for any use that may be made of the information it contains.

---

[3] **E**ducation for **D**ata **I**ntensive **S**cience to **O**pen **N**ew Science Frontiers.

References

1. Angelini, M., Catarci, T., Mecella, M., Santucci, G.: Visual analytics and mining over big data. Discussing some issues and challenges, and presenting a few experiences. In: Bornschlegl et al. [5], pp. 363–367. http://doi.acm.org/10.1145/2909132.2927471

2. Ardito, C., Buono, P., Costabile, M.F., Desolda, G., Matera, M.: A meta-design approach to support information access and manipulation in virtual research environments. In: Bornschlegl et al. [5], pp. 363–367. http://doi.acm.org/10.1145/2909132.2927471

3. Bornschlegl, M.X.: Data science competences to understand big data analysis from a management perspective - a top down view. In: Hemmje et al. [15]

4. Bornschlegl, M.X., Berwind, K., Kaufmann, M., Hemmje, M.L.: Towards a reference model for advanced visual interfaces supporting big data analysis. In: Proceedings on the International Conference on Internet Computing (ICOMP), The Steering Committee of The World Congress in Computer Science, Computer Engineering and Applied Computing (WorldComp), Las Vegas, Nevada, USA, pp. 78–81 (2016)

5. Bornschlegl, M.X., Manieri, A., Walsh, P., Catarci, T., Hemmje, M.L.: Road mapping infrastructures for advanced visual interfaces supporting big data applications in virtual research environments. In: Buono et al. [6], pp. 363–367. http://doi.acm.org/10.1145/2909132.2927471

6. Buono, P., Lanzilotti, R., Matera, M., Costabile, M.F. (eds.): Proceedings of the International Working Conference on Advanced Visual Interfaces, AVI 2016, Bari, Italy, June 7–10, 2016. ACM (2016). http://doi.acm.org/10.1145/2909132

7. Card, S.K., Mackinlay, J.D., Shneiderman, B. (eds.): Readings in Information Visualization: Using Vision to Think. Morgan Kaufmann Publishers Inc., San Francisco (1999)

8. Danowski, C., Bornschlegl, M.X., Schmidt, B., Hemmje, M.L.: Modern technologies to synchronize data sources and information visualizations. In: Bornschlegl et al. [5], pp. 363–367. http://doi.acm.org/10.1145/2909132.2927471

9. Day, J., Cantwell, M.: Citizen initiated river basin planning: the salmon watershed example. Environments **25**(2/3), 80 (1998). [salmon river watershed round table]

10. Engel, F., Bond, R., Keary, A., Mulvenna, M., Walsh, P., Hiuru, Z., Kowohl, U., Hemmje, M.L.: Sensecare: towards an experimental platform for home-based, visualisation of emotional states of people with dementia. In: Bornschlegl et al. [5], pp. 363–367. http://doi.acm.org/10.1145/2909132.2927471

11. Commission, E.: Education for data intensive science to open new science frontiers. H2020-INFRASUPP-2015-1, Proposal number: 675419, Proposal acronym: EDISON (2015)

12. Fischer, G.: Context-aware systems: the 'right' information, at the 'right' time, in the 'right' place, in the 'right' way, to the 'right' person. In: Proceedings of the International Working Conference on Advanced Visual Interfaces, AVI 2012, pp. 287–294. ACM, New York (2012)

13. Fraunhofer Institute for Computer Graphics Research IGD: Visual business analytics (2015). http://www.igd.fraunhofer.de/en/Institut/Abteilungen/Informationsvisualisierung-und-Visual-Analytics/Visual-Business-Analytics. Accessed 02 Dec 2015

14. Harrison, J., Uhomoibhi, J.O.: Engineering study of tidal stream renewable energy generation and visualization: issues of process modelling and implementation. In: Bornschlegl et al. [5], pp. 363–367. http://doi.acm.org/10.1145/2909132.2927471

15. Hemmje, M.L., Brocks, H., Becker, J. (eds.): Demand Of Data Science Skills & Competences (Expert Roundtable), November 2015
16. Kaufmann, M.: Towards a reference model for big data management. Research report, forthcoming(2016)
17. Manieri, A., Demchenko, Y., Wiktorski, T., Brewer, S., Hemmje, M., Ferrari, T., Riestra, R., Frey, J.: Data science professional uncovered - how the edison project will contribute to a widely accepted profile for data scientists (2015)
18. Nonaka, I., Takeuchi, H.: The knowledge-creating company: how Japanese companies create the dynamics of innovation. Oxford University Press (1995)
19. Onime, C., Uhomoibhi, J.O.: Cost effective visualization of research data for cognitive development using mobile augmented reality. In: Bornschlegl et al. [5], pp. 363–367. http://doi.acm.org/10.1145/2909132.2927471
20. Riggas, D., Ashton, S., de Angelis, K., Graf, C.: How to plan, organize, perform, evaluate and document roundtables. European Comission, The Directorate-General for Education and Culture (DG EAC) (2010). https://cocoate.com/sites/cocoate.com/files/guide.pdf
21. Sharp, H., Rogers, Y., Preece, J.: Interaction Design: Beyond Human Computer Interaction. Wiley, New York (2007)
22. Swoboda, T., Nawroth, C., Kaufmann, M.: Towards interactive visualization of results from domain specific text analytics. In: Bornschlegl et al. [5], pp. 363–367. http://doi.acm.org/10.1145/2909132.2927471
23. Upadhyay, S., Grant, R.: 5 data scientists who became CEOS and are leading thriving companies. http://venturebeat.com/2013/12/03/5-data-scientists-who-became-ceos-and-are-leading-thriving-companies/. Accessed 30 Oct 2015
24. Walsh, P., Lawlor, B., Kelly, B., Bekaert, M., Manning, T., Heuss, T., Lu, X., Sleator, R., Leopold, M.: Rapidly visualizing NGS cancer data sets with cloud computing. In: Bornschlegl et al. [5], pp. 363–367. http://doi.acm.org/10.1145/2909132.2927471
25. Zeepedia: Evaluation paradigms and techniques (2010). http://www.zeepedia.com/read.php?evaluation_paradigms_and_techniques_human_computer_interaction&b=11&c=29. Accessed 01 July 2016

Author Index

.

Printed in the United States
by Baker & Taylor Publisher Services